**TAKE
YOURSELF
TO THE
TOP**

▼

ARE YOU READY TO . . .
TAKE YOURSELF TO THE TOP?

▲ Are you willing to develop personally to get where you want to be professionally?

▲ Do you want a higher quality of life along with more financial rewards?

▲ Are you open to new ways of doing things?

▲ Are you free of fixations that could cripple your career?

▲ Do you have the time and resources to invest in yourself?

TAKE YOURSELF TO THE TOP

▼

Success from the Inside Out

LAURA BERMAN FORTGANG

Jeremy P. Tarcher/Penguin
a member of Penguin Group (USA) Inc.
New York

JEREMY P. TARCHER/PENGUIN
Published by the Penguin Group
Penguin Group (USA) Inc., 375 Hudson Street, New York, New York 10014, USA • Penguin
Group (Canada), 90 Eglinton Avenue East, Suite 700, Toronto, Ontario M4P 2Y3, Canada (a division
of Pearson Penguin Canada Inc.) • Penguin Books Ltd, 80 Strand, London WC2R 0RL, England
• Penguin Ireland, 25 St Stephen's Green, Dublin 2, Ireland (a division of Penguin Books Ltd) •
Penguin Group (Australia), 250 Camberwell Road, Camberwell, Victoria 3124, Australia (a division
of Pearson Australia Group Pty Ltd) • Penguin Books India Pvt Ltd, 22 Community Centre,
Panchsheel Park, New Delhi–110 017, India • Penguin Group (NZ), Cnr Airborne and Rosedale
Roads, Albany, Auckland 1310, New Zealand (a division of Pearson New Zealand Ltd) • Penguin
Books (South Africa) (Pty) Ltd, 24 Sturdee Avenue, Rosebank, Johannesburg 2196, South Africa •
Penguin Books Ltd, Registered Offices: 80 Strand, London WC2R 0RL, England

First published in 1998 by Warner Books
First Jeremy P. Tarcher/Penguin edition 2005
Copyright © 1998, 2005 by Laura Berman Fortgang

Most Tarcher/Penguin books are available at special quantity discounts for bulk purchase for
sales promotions, premiums, fund-raising, and educational needs. Special books or book excerpts
also can be created to fit specific needs. For details, write Penguin Group (USA) Inc.
Special Markets, 375 Hudson Street, New York, NY 10014

Library of Congress Cataloging-in-Publication Data

Fortgang, Laura Berman.
Take yourself to the top : success from the inside out /
Laura Berman Fortgang.—1st Jeremy P. Tarcher/Penguin ed.
p.   cm.
ISBN 1-58542-447-1
1. Career development.   2. Career changes.   I. Title.
HF5381.F683   2005   2005041826
650.14—dc22

Printed in the United States of America
1   3   5   7   9   10   8   6   4   2

Book design by Charles Sutherland

While the author has made every effort to provide accurate telephone numbers and Internet
addresses at the time of publication, neither the publisher nor the author assumes any responsibility for errors or for changes that occur after publication. Further, the publisher does not have
any control over and does not assume any responsibility for third-party Web sites or their content.

This book is dedicated to all my clients—past, present, and future—who allow me the privilege of partnership in their lives and careers, and to my father, whose career inspired my beliefs and ambitions.

Author's Note

To give an author the opportunity to revise an older work is an exciting and rare treat. *Take Yourself to the Top* was written in 1997 and published in 1998, and was my very first book. So much has happened to the coaching profession since then, and certainly my work with clients has morphed over the years. There is no question that more people have heard of professional coaching now than in 1998. However, the biggest change is the world we live in.

Our world is less secure. Our trust in the institutions that have shaped our lives is in question. Our subsequent re-evaluation of how we want to live has put many of us in flux. None of this is a tragedy; it's just new and it can make us uncomfortable. And yet, in my definition, discomfort equals growth. We are being asked to stretch way outside of our comfort zone. My wish is that our stretch will lead to extraordinary innovation and evolution as people and as a global community. I sincerely hope this book will assist you in yours.

Laura Berman Fortgang
October 2004

Acknowledgments

BEFORE I EVEN BEGAN WRITING THIS BOOK, I HAD STARTED A mental list of the people I had to acknowledge for their contribution to it and to the journey that led me to write it. To all of you, and to those whom I may have forgotten to mention, a heartfelt thank-you for your time, inspiration, expertise, and support.

Sheila Kutner of The Showplace in Philadelphia, my first mentor, who took me under her wing and introduced me to the world of corporate training. What a gift your interest in me has been.

Thomas Leonard, my next mentor, who introduced me to coaching as a model for the work I wanted to do with people. You gave language to a lifetime of things I knew to be true and did not yet know how to express. Thank you.

Sandy Vilas, president of Coach University, for the opportunities you have generously shared with me.

Jay Perry, Marlene Elliot, and especially Cheryl Richardson, trusted coaching colleagues who shared their best with me and invested in my ability to achieve.

Dr. Charlee Garden, Lucy Rosen, and Jacquette Timmons, talented consultants in their own right who have shared their expertise and contacts generously with me.

The Coach's Council, a group of the most talented coaches in the country, who get together to support each other personally and professionally. Thank you for being the best in the business and a great source of inspiration.

Madeleine Homan, who gave countless hours of her time to this project by reading, editing, challenging, and policing my efforts. Thank you for your humor, wit, encouragement, generosity, great ideas, and contributions.

Rick Wolff, my editor at Warner Books, who taught me how to bring my voice to the page and who coached me, in his own way, to bring out my best. Thank you for teaching me the ropes.

At William Morris, my thanks to my agent, Mel Berger, and his assistant, Claudia Cross, as well as Phil Liebowitz, whose lifetime of support has not gone unnoticed.

In its revision and continued long life, this book would not be possible without the loving care of my publishing home, Tarcher Penguin. The unsurpassed support of my publisher, Joel Fotinos; the care of my editor, Sara Carder, and her assistant, Ashley Shelby; the chutzpah of Kelly Groves and Katie Grinch in publicity; and the creativity and muscle of the sales team are treasures whose rare value I appreciate. Equally important has been the championing provided by my current agent, Joelle Delbourgo, and her team of associates. Thank you all.

At InterCoach, my thanks to all teams past and present, and especially Jeanne B.

All the clients who have taken time to endorse me and care about me personally, and especially Mary Jane Range, whose willingness to go to the media with her coaching success story made a huge difference in my life. I am grateful to all of you.

To countless friends, colleagues, and family that have contributed to my support, thank you.

To my parents, who have been the foundation and always present support in my life, thank you. A special thanks to Fran Berman, my mother, a great friend and a keen editor, who has endured many a creative project with me.

And last, but not least, thank you to my husband, Mark Fortgang, for his cyber/techno savvy and, most important, for the love that has opened me up to my potential.

Contents

Introduction

TAKE YOURSELF TO THE TOP. WHAT DOES THAT MEAN TO YOU? What game is worth spending your precious energy on? What if that game were the game of your life? Take yourself to the top of your life! That has a nice ring to it. Whether you're on a corporate career track or you're an entrepreneur, your work will define a lot of that game. If you design that part with your whole life in mind, you'll get it right and be able to call the shots. Let me introduce you to something that will help.

In picking up this book, you've picked up your own personal coach. I am going to help you take your personal and professional life to the next level. You will be introduced to new concepts and ideas and reminded of some old ones, but all in a new context. That context is *coaching*. Coaching takes an inside-out approach to your career success. As someone once said, "It's not the way things are, it's the way *we* are." This book will show you how to change in order to get the outside circumstances of your life and career to change. We'll unlock your potential by help-ing you grow and investing in your ability to achieve. We will usher in the success that you have been waiting for, but not nec-essarily the one you had in mind.

If you're looking for typical job search or career hunting advice, this is not the book for you. I will not cover résumé writing, cover letters, interviewing skills, or dressing for success. I won't fuss with a lot of busywork. But if you're a successful person who is ready to take your executive or entrepreneurial success to the next level, you've come to the right place. I don't mince words. I keep people from believing the baloney they make up about themselves. My tone has been called "edgy," and my clients say they pay me to tell them the truth. That willingness to hear the truth and try new ways of doing things has taken many of them to where they have wanted to go and beyond. They know that I believe they can do what they have set out to do, until they prove me wrong. They are assured that I won't step over anything that could be pointed out as something they could improve. Anger is not a tool I use to mo-tivate my clients. I am amused, however, by how our own human nature makes us choose less than ideal circumstances for our lives, and I am not afraid to point out such ironies to my clients in a very blunt way.

To get ideas that will help you take yourself to the top, you'll read about Sarah, who came to coaching to help her build her business within a recruiting firm. In eighteen months her in-come grew from $65,000 to $500,000. You'll also read about Jay, an entrepreneur who made his home-based business grow from a hobby to a million-dollar-a-year enterprise. Britt was a vice president who became a national director after seven weeks of applying what she learned from being coached. If these exam-ples are far from where you are now, don't worry. You'll get valuable information that you can apply to your own journey.

A lot of the success stories should inspire you, and some stories will be less sunny, to point out that not everyone is ready to hear what a coach might say. This book is for you if you're ready to take charge of your career as you never have before. If you think you're a victim, you're not ready for what is ahead.

The concepts and tips in this book will be useful, but you'll have to create a structure in which to assimilate them. This book won't give you the structure that working with a coach can provide; you'll have to do that for yourself. The chapter on self-discipline will help. When I work with my clients, we have weekly half-hour or hour sessions, usually by phone, on an ongoing basis. We work together for at least ninety days, with a nine-month average stay for most people. Those who really apply themselves to their coaching stay longer, two years or more.

Michael Gerber, who wrote *The E Myth,* says that entrepreneurs must work *on* their business instead of just *in* it. He observed that most people, entrepreneurs or not, spend more time doing what they do than planning and designing it. When people take the time to plan, the doing becomes much easier. That idea has been adopted in client coaching. Whether you are growing a business, designing your corporate career track, or working to achieve a balance in your life, working weekly with a coach allows you the structure and the time to work *on* your life instead of just being *in* it.

I often compare getting results from coaching to getting results at the gym. You can join and keep paying your money, but if you don't go and do the work, you don't get the bod. It's the same with coaching: You use the coach to get you where you want to go. If you don't show up and you don't do the work, then you'll be doing what you've always done and getting the usual results. To get the most out of this book, work it! Read it, do the exercises, and apply them immediately. Don't let this be another book with good ideas that you do nothing about. Be someone who values him- or herself enough to do so. Visit this book often, even after you've finished, and let it coach you.

This book will work for you regardless of what industry you work or run your business in. The same goes for coaching. Some clients prefer to work with a coach who shares an industry expertise with them. That has to do with their comfort; it doesn't necessarily make coaching more effective. It's not an industry-specific discipline, it's a people-specific discipline. The time it takes for you to adapt this material will depend on who you are and whether or not you are coachable. Are you over the hump financially? Are you free of any addictions or conditions that could cripple your life? Are you willing to develop yourself personally so you can get where you want to go professionally? Are you open to new ways of doing things? Do you want a higher quality of life, with more financial rewards as well? Do you have the time and resources to invest in yourself? If you answered yes to these questions, we're a match. If you didn't, what are you willing to do to get yourself there?

If you've picked up this book, you're probably facing a career concern or frustration, or you are ready for the next step and not quite sure how to get there. I wonder if you're leafing through these pages discreetly in a bookstore aisle or if you're sequestered in the privacy of your own home. When clients first find me as you've found this book, they often consider their coach their "secret weapon" or are embarrassed that they need this kind of partnership at all. So if that has crossed your mind, get over it fast. What is the shame of having a partner who is 100 percent devoted to your success? Can you do it alone? Absolutely. Can you do it better with someone to hold you accountable, cheer you on, point out pitfalls, build on your strengths, and help you chart out your path? Yes. So why should you be embarrassed?

Are You Ready, Willing, and Able to Be Coached?

Ready

1. I have time to invest in myself.   Yes____ No____

2. I can make and keep appointments
   with myself to work on this material.   Yes____ No____

3. There is a gap between where I am
   and where I want to be.   Yes____ No____

Willing

4. I am fully willing to do the work
   required to get me where I want to go.   Yes____ No____

5. I am willing to stop or change the self-
   defeating behaviors that limit my success.   Yes____ No____

6. I am willing to try new things even if I am
   not 100 percent convinced they will work.   Yes____ No____

Able

7. Coaching is the appropriate discipline
   for the changes I want to make (rather
   than therapy or a twelve-step program).   Yes____ No____

8. I have the patience to take consistent
   action toward my goals, regardless of
   how immediate the results are.   Yes____ No____

9. I have the support I need to make
   significant changes with ease
   (i.e., family or company buy-in).   Yes____ No____

If you answered no to two or more of these questions, you will need to make adjustments before the coaching can be effective.

"Why can't a friend or a spouse do this for me?" I've been asked many times. They can, but only to a certain degree. Family and friends lack the objectivity that a coach can provide and, more important, they have an agenda different from your coach's. Your success or growth in a new direction can be threatening to someone whose relationship to you depends on your staying basically the way you are. Of course, your loved ones want you to be happy and fulfilled, but even positive change can be an unforeseen threat to the status quo. Your coach is not threatened by your success; that is your coach's only agenda. It's a different kind of relationship and a different kind of support.

Since coaching is a new profession that is both similar to and yet so different from some others, it might help to spell out where the similarities and differences are. Coaching is hot right now, and many consultants are calling themselves coaches. Here are the three most common comparisons:

Career Coach vs. Career Counselor—A coach's main job is to help you to take action to close the gap between where you are and where you want to be. A career counselor may be the perfect person to help you figure out where you want to be. Counselors can administer personality and capability assessments and help you determine what is an appropriate career for you. A coach might help you determine your next step, but is more likely to help you do so by exploring your needs and what you truly value in life. The client usually has a pretty good idea of what might be next and uses the coach to design a strategy to get there and to include the new direction in a complete life plan/design.

Coach vs. Business Consultant—A consultant is likely to be an expert in your specific business and be more hands-on than a coach might be. You hire consultants to fix or enhance your business, and you pay them for their advice and work. They will tell you what to do, but a coach is more likely to ask you a lot of questions to get you to come up with your own answers. Of course, coaches have hundreds of tools to help you make your business grow, create better systems, and develop your people, but they are more likely to design it with you than for you. Many coaches are consultants, but not all consultants are coaches. Many consultants I have coached have said, "You get down to a much more personal level with people to help them overcome the obstacles in their business; I could never get that close to my clients."

Coach vs. Psychotherapist—I would never dream of performing therapy on my clients. I don't have a license to do so. Therapists address major emotional issues and try to help clients find context and understanding, based on the past. If a client is in emotional pain, therapy is a better choice than coaching. Coaches will take business and personal issues and explore them in a framework that is action-oriented. We want to help our clients create great futures. We work to get them over hurdles by finding out what needs to be added or taken away and by doing so as quickly as possible. We look for the source of obstacles as a therapist might, but do not deal in introspection. Often, coaching will cause clients to realize they need therapy if it becomes clear that the coach has uncovered an issue that does not lend itself to a coaching solution.

As your coach, I'll become your partner and take you to the next level, but I'll never allow the goal to become more important than your well-being as a person. Coaching is holistic. When we work on your career goals, our work is held in the context of how those goals reflect who you are as a person and fit into what will work for your whole life. Taking yourself to the top is not about reaching your goals at any cost. It's not about clawing your way to the top of the ladder. That is how people screw up their lives. Taking yourself to the top is about defining success on your own terms and designing your professional and personal life to reflect that.

So let's get to work. This book cannot replace the human dynamic of the coach/client partnership, but it can give you insight into yourself and the path to your next level of success.

How to Use This Book

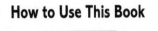

1. Seek out the chapters that address your situation.
2. Go back and read them all. Each chapter holds clues to your success, regardless of your situation or field.
3. Stop and do the exercises. You'll learn a lot about yourself.
4. Use a piece of paper or pad headed "Action Plan" to record the changes you would like to make.
5. After finishing the book, prioritize your action plan, and you'll have a blueprint for your personal and professional development.

ONE

Where You Were, Where You Are Now, and Overcoming the Hurdles to Where You Want to Go

"It's not like it used to be."

Every generation has a time it remembers as "the good old days," and it seems that we are no different. I suppose it depends on how old you are as you read this, but the bulk of my clients reminisce about the early eighties, when there was a boom, and then again the mid-to-late nineties, when we had a nice run of economic flourish. Of course, we can't forget the big hiccups in between. The 1987 market crash in the United States led to some long periods of unemployment as well as corporate restructuring, and September 11, 2001, brought devastation financially, emotionally, and spiritually, and a resulting war. If your life has been affected by these events or any since that time, you are probably asking yourself some important questions. No matter what your circumstances, in picking up this book you are probably asking yourself, What do I really want? What's going to make me happy?

Our entire culture in the twenty-first century is going through a shift believing that they are entitled to liking what they do and having a higher quality of life. Past generations rarely considered being happy a part of the work scenario. You did what you needed to do to provide for your family and that was that. No one talked about being fulfilled at the same time. We now believe it is possible (and preferable) to enjoy the bulk of our waking hours, which are spent working and earning.

It makes sense that coaching emerged in the 1990s as a tool for people to redesign their work in the process of creating more fulfilling lives. The kick in the mid-nineties to "get a life" and find a work-life balance began what has now become a demand for more meaningful work. Coaching as a new profession, which is distinct from psychotherapy and business consulting, fills the need for guidance on how to achieve this. You would think that it would be easy enough for any one of us to figure this puzzle out by ourselves, but in reality, that is not the case. We are in transition from the old-world work ethic into the new-world work ethic. We have few models to follow and the culture is divided in terms of readiness. Not everyone is ready to have it all (meaning and satisfaction as well as resources for living). The real question then becomes, What will it take for you to be ready?

We are not meant to suffer to make a living. However, if that still feels out of reach for you or you are going through a tough time, please know that the concept won't be foreign to you for long. If you really take a look at corporate downsizing, the exporting of certain industries that used to employ many Americans, and the caution that companies are exercising in hiring, you can see that we are being given a hidden opportunity even though it presents itself as a bad situation. The hidden opportunity in a tighter economy and interestingly enough in boom times as well is the opportunity to reinvent—to correct some things you put up with before and to get back in touch with your core values, to what matters to you most.

You may find yourself questioning how you were successful before and wondering how to re-create that in a world that doesn't work the same way. This is where your core values come in. The answer is to get at who you are and what you care about and reorient your world around these criteria. You will be shedding the criteria for success that you inherited or that you have come to accept as society has dictated it to you, and you will discover your own definition of success, your own definition of what the top is.

It is no wonder that small business has been a continually growing segment of business in this country. Many want to give a shot to doing things their own way.

This brings me to the reasons that this book is directed at both corporate types and entrepreneurs. To the naked eye they look like opposites; not true at all—you have a lot to learn from each other. You may once have been two different breeds, but you are coming together as one species that will work hand in hand. Corporate America has changed. You will no longer expect to be loyal to one company for your whole career, in exchange for its loyalty to you. You have to think like an entrepreneur; in these times, you will change jobs often during your career. It has been said that you no longer work for a company at all; you work for yourself. Your career is your own company, to which you keep adding credentials, skills, knowledge, and experience, to prepare it for an IPO. You want to make yourself so valuable that the headhunters are tearing down your door, and companies are having bidding wars to get you. You will have to do that for yourself. No company will do it for you—at least, not anymore.

Some of you have jumped the corporate ship and gone out on your own; everything you learned inside will help you outside. Others have always been self-employed. Whether you're a veteran or a newcomer, you face the challenge of sustaining a profitable venture without corporate-sized budgets. You are constantly challenged to become smarter and more resourceful. You carry the burden of keeping the business alive and still finding time to see your family. You are on the front line every day.

As executives and entrepreneurs, you share an ability to see the big picture; you have a penchant for making an impact and seeing your efforts create big results. Others look to you to give them direction, and you have the capacity to leave a legacy that determines how business and organizations work. Your power is unlimited, yet you run into obstacles along the way that stall or distract you. This book will walk you through each one and get you to the other side. You have a job to do: to make your life the way you want it. That is what it means to be a leader. That is what it means to truly be at the top—fully actualized, fully satisfied, fully using all your capabilities. Your feelings about work, and your level of success in that area, color so many parts of your world. They affect what you bring to your home life and your community. This works the other way around too, but since you spend so much of your time at work, shouldn't it be great?

What's stopping you from taking yourself to the top? The clients that I have been privileged to work with over the last few years have represented ten career/life hurdles that needed to be overcome. Let's take an overview of what they are, to prepare you to work through those that affect you. You'll need to be ready to drop all your whining and complaining if you want to get through them. The choice is really up to you: Will you master your life, or will it master you? Will you allow circumstances to take control, or will you dictate the terms? You are a leader; leaders take charge. Take charge of your career, and take charge of your life. If you don't feel up to it, put this book away until you are ready. Just reading won't do you any good; you'll have to DO something about it!

DO ANY OF THESE SOUND FAMILIAR?

1) **You're midcareer, and you're feeling stuck.** You've hit a dead end, and you think there is no way out. Think again. We'll create a rumbling (or even an earthquake) in your world and get things moving again.

2) **You're on a never-ending treadmill, and you feel like you can't get off.** Oh, you poor workaholic, you. A life of over-achievement. You've got enough to be proud of; now it's time to live. We'll adjust your perception to bring a balance to your life.

3) **You really want to be doing something else.** How long are you going to let it eat at you? We'll help you honor what you long to do, and we'll overcome every reason that you think means you can't make a change.

4) **You're stuck in survival mode.** Business is stalled. You've un-derestimated yourself and given up too soon. We'll get you comfortable with pushing the envelope.

5) **You're new at entrepreneurship.** An exciting new life! So full of promise, so full of pitfalls. We'll shorten your learning curve and get you up to speed.

6) **You're at the mercy of the ups and downs of sales.** What a miserable existence; no fun at all. If you get out of the trap of

needing the sale, many more of them will start rolling in. We'll take you to a new level of awareness about yourself, and we'll show you how this works.

7) You feel overqualified and underutilized. If you want drama in your life, this is one way to get it. Let's get you out in front and shining. You'll get noticed, but not by doing what you think will work. We'll stretch you beyond the limits you think the job has put on you.

8) You think you have to be the Hero. You're overwhelmed; there is too much to do. You've probably taken on more than you need to. We'll teach you the skills that will motivate you and your staff to a higher level of performance. As a result, you'll be free to excel, and you'll feel like you have time on your hands.

9) You're having an identity crisis. The times have changed and yet you may not be willing to change with them. Or perhaps the changing roles of men and women in the workplace and at home are making things confusing. Or maybe you have to figure out your next steps and you are stuck. It's time to get out of your stubbornness and respond to the truth about what is going on around you. You have to dig out your heels and become flexible in order to gain a new self-concept, or you'll stay in pain and stuck. We'll usher you through to the real you and get you to the other side of the crisis.

10) You're waiting for a miracle. Hoping will get you nowhere. Taking responsibility will start to get you somewhere closer to reality. If you ignore the signs that you or your business are in trouble, this will only cause you greater trouble down the road. We'll teach you to recognize the signs so you can turn yourself around.

It doesn't matter what package your frustrations come in. Most of you just want to make more money and be happy; that's all you ask. It sounds simple enough. If I could bottle a tonic and serve it to you by the spoonful, I would. But for now, coaching is the best solution I've found. So gear up to do whatever it takes to get what you want.

If you're facing a specific obstacle, you will be led to direct solutions. If you are still not sure what is keeping you from taking yourself to the top, determine what the gap is. Where would you like to be? Read with that inquiry in mind, and you'll pick up steps to get you there. You may find yourself facing a combination of hurdles; that's not unusual. Just don't let it stop you; it's not a crime, but not doing something about them is. If you've come this far, you have no other choice but to go through with it. You have a coach now. Let me help you bring out your best.

You can have it all. But are you ready?

Get Started

1. Assess where you are now.
2. Identify specifically where you want to be.
3. Use the exercises to move you forward.
4. Pause after each chapter, and write down what you will add to your "action plan."
5. Give up excuses!
6. Take charge. Take action!

TWO

Midcareer and Feeling Stuck. Will You Ever Get Ahead?

"It's an impossible situation. I can't see my way out of this, and I have no idea what to do next."

DAVID WAS IN HIS MIDFORTIES AND HAD BEEN WITH THE SAME company for fifteen years. He had been in his position as a senior manager for four years when he came to work with me. He felt stuck, and he was not very clear about what he wanted to accomplish by hiring a coach. He did know that he was willing to take action to get unstuck, and he hoped I could lend some direction to that process. He thought that he had reached the top rung of his career path in this company, and he felt that he was at the end of the road. He didn't want to think that there was nothing to look forward to, but for the moment, that was the truth.

As it turned out, he had every reason to feel stuck, but things weren't as hopeless as he made it sound. He was encumbered by a difficult boss and a backlog of personal and professional projects, and he carried some emotional baggage from a divorce a few years earlier. I asked him to work out some of the divorce issues with a therapist, and I coached him through the process of reevaluating and completing his backlog of unfinished projects. The personal projects on his list included getting back to some hobbies he missed, getting some overdue work done on his apartment, and recommitting to a fitness regime. These things started to give him renewed energy, and he began to shed the feeling of being stuck.

On the professional side, many of David's projects at work were unfinished because his boss squelched every idea he came up with. We worked on some communication skills to improve the situation with his boss. We determined what boundaries he needed to put in place to keep this person from having a negative effect on him. He stopped letting his boss dump projects and problems on him, and got him to stop using an authoritarian style. Once all this was out of the way, David was lighter in his mood and clearer about what had been missing for him. He saw that he had been so stifled that he was no longer doing what he loved best, which was coming up with ideas. He was so used to being ignored that he had stopped trying.

There was no question that what was next for him was to get back to doing what he was good at. I asked him to share his ideas at every meeting for the following thirty days. It did not take long for him to start getting the attention he deserved. He emerged as a leader in the organization, and within four months of our beginning to work together, he was offered one of the top three positions in the company as the "idea" person, the head of Research and Development.

*   *   *

If you are feeling stuck, you've got only yourself to thank. It means you missed signs that a change was due. You ignored the signs that were loudly screaming, "No, try something else!"—not necessarily a new job, but a new strategy, tack, or latent skill. If you feel stuck, somewhere along the way you decided to put up with a lot—for whatever reason—and you have started sinking deeper and deeper into the Unconscious Zone. This is the place where you lie down and let life run over you; you ignore what you know is true because it is easier to put up with it than to actually DO something about it. You missed the message. It turned into a problem, and you still ignored it. Then it became a lesson you did not learn, so now you've got a crisis on your hands. You're unhappy, and that affects everything in your life. You probably could make a very strong case about why things are the way they are, and a list a mile long of who is to blame. Of course, if your name is on it at all, it's only penciled in.

OK, that's enough browbeating. It's time to do something about it. You haven't been giving yourself your best lately, but now is the time to start. I want your best, or I want nothing. No, I take it back. You were doing the best you could—but now is the time to go for it. Are you ready?

First, we need to take a look at the clutter you have let build up in your life—the stuff you have put up with that we are going to deem unacceptable in about two minutes. All that stuff is like tar on a hot road, making your feet stick to the pavement. It's slowing you down and holding you back. That stuff could be things you are unresolved about from the past, certain present circumstances or damaging influences that you have chosen to endure. This is exactly what is keeping you stuck. You'll have to identify this clutter and remove it to move on to greener pastures.

CLEARING THE SLATE

Without further ado, take out a piece of paper and make two columns on it. (Do it. Don't just read this part and keep going. Do this!) The column on the left should read: "Things that hold me up at work." The column on the right should say: "Things that hold me up at home." Once you have at least ten items in each column, start eliminating each thing, one by one. This might be as simple as a messy filing system, or as complicated as a political structure in your company. Start with the easy ones first, and work your way up to the hard ones.

As you get rid of things, you should start feeling more and more optimistic or at least start understanding more clearly what your next steps are going to be. Once you get down to the final tough ones, you probably will have some big decisions to make. For example, you might be left with an item that is unresolvable, and this may mean leaving your present position altogether. Don't panic. Just ask yourself what you want for your life, and what you have to do will become undeniable. Remember: No more denial; that's what got you stuck in the first place.

I recently had a conversation with a client about this. I asked him point-blank "to tolerate nothing." I could almost feel his eyes widen over the phone. He never knew he had the right to do that. As the head of a department that depended on many other departments to do its job, he put up with a lot of incompetencies. Something clicked for him, though, when I asked him to try this tactic. Within a couple of weeks, he had met with all the right people and had found solutions that would eliminate the annoyances he had put up with. He started to see that his job had become impossible because he himself had allowed it to become impossible. He is now full of energy and eager to tackle his job every day, instead of feeling that it is an unproductive dead end that he may have to leave. Now, when something comes up, he eliminates the problem right away and avoids putting up with anything for long.

As you are clearing up your list, keep in mind the following tools and concepts that might help you. Not everyone who works on getting unstuck has to change jobs or careers, but getting unstuck definitely means making changes. One of those changes will be putting boundaries in place that insulate you from some of the garbage you've been putting up with. Do people interrupt you when you speak? Do people infringe on your time? Do certain people talk to you in a way that is offensive? Do other people take credit for your ideas? Do you keep saying yes to project after project, increasing your time at work by hour after hour? If the answer to any of these questions is yes, it's time to extend your boundaries.

Boundaries are imaginary lines that keep other people's actions and behaviors out. Anything that causes you to get annoyed or upset is a crossed boundary. You've let your boundaries collapse. If you had a swimming pool in your backyard without a fence around it, you might find all kinds of unwelcome guests splashing around in it. When a sturdy fence is in place, what happens? People have to ask permission to jump in; they have to be invited. You are the pool; the fence is your boundary. Don't let anyone jump in your pool without permission. In its simplest form, a boundary is the word *NO!*

Here's an example: A sales rep who was well liked in his office left his door open, and all who felt like chatting just made themselves at home there and shot the breeze with him. He always enjoyed these interactions, but didn't know how to get people out of his office politely so he could get his work done. Over time, he got less and less done at work, which caused him to do more and more at home, which in turn made his family angry with him. By the time he hired me to help him get back on track, he was stressed, overwhelmed, and unproductive. He had collapsed his boundaries with his colleagues completely. He let them monopolize his time, and then he contorted himself to make up for it. He had to put strict boundaries around his time, and he also had to reeducate people, teaching them how to find out when he was ready to have some downtime. People now had to ask, and they could not assume that he was always available. He put a boundary in place that dictated how others needed to act around him.

Another client had the kind of high-energy, quick-paced job that included constant phone interaction. The ongoing interruptions of the phone calls caused her to feel like she never got anything done, and, as a result, she began to work late into the evening. She fought me for a long time, but finally agreed to try putting a boundary around her time on the phone. Instead of allowing constant interruptions, she started letting her assistant take messages, and every ninety minutes she would stop and return calls. The result was that she had much more focused time to accomplish her work, and her phone calls were more focused because they were no longer the nuisance they had been.

Boundaries need to be put in place to keep any damaging influences out of your way. Those influences may be circumstances you created or that someone else's actions have created for you. Someone's tone of voice, level of negativity, or propensity for criticism, among other things, may cause you to need boundaries, to protect yourself and your goals from disruptive influences. Remember: You are not putting up with anything anymore, which means that you'll probably have to reeducate some people if they are going to stay around you. Interpersonal boundaries are invisible; you have to communicate them for them to be known. If other people can't comply, you may have to make an effort to avoid them altogether.

Put Your Boundaries in Place

1. Stop people just as they are doing something that violates your boundary.
2. Tell them what they are doing.
3. Request that they stop.
4. Instruct them about the change you need to see.
5. Thank them for making the change.

If they are not cooperative, add 6 or 7.

6. *Demand* that they stop.
7. Walk away without a fight.

The bottom line is that "they" are not doing anything to you that you are not allowing them to do.

You may need to fire some people from your life. This may mean literally firing people in a business situation, if that is appropriate and substantiated, but, more important, it means firing people emotionally. You will no longer be investing in them or in your relationship with them. If people cannot respond to honest feedback and direct requests to change something, then they are not willing to change and are no longer your problem. My rule is: Three strikes and you're out. Look, we can't change other people—we can only change ourselves. The only way to make progress, once you've tried unsuccessfully to work things out, is to get out. If you don't do this, you will only have more dead weight holding you back from what you want. It will keep you from having room in your life for the people who do bring out your best.

Think about it: What three things get in your way most often that a boundary could help alleviate? Put your new boundaries in place. Boundaries won't work if other people don't know they are there.

In David's case, once he had the proper boundaries in place with his boss, getting the position that he really wanted finally came down to getting back in touch with what he was good at. Getting stuck often has a lot to do with forgetting why you do what you do, or what attracted you to it in the first place. If you're too far away from that, you will be dissatisfied. Other times, you just may have outgrown your job altogether, and there may be no place to use your talents. In the first situation, you need to get back to doing what you love, and in the other, you need to find out where your strengths have developed and find a new place to use them.

Get in touch with what turns you on. Maybe you're toward the top of your game. Perhaps you're a VP of sales. You don't exactly love it, because you are many steps removed from what attracted you to sales in the first place: meeting the client, making the presentation, closing the sale. Should you demote yourself to get back there? No. Maybe you can go out more on calls with your reps to keep in touch with sales, or you can start a small side business so you can get a taste of it again. Just dare to do what you love; dare to be creative to be happy.

Treasure Hunt

Ask five people you trust to tell you what they think your greatest professional strengths are. Then ask them what they think your natural gifts are. Do your professional strengths match your natural talents? Find a way to integrate them both into what you do for a living. It may help you determine why you have not been playing full-out or why you are not being noticed for all you can do. You weren't honoring yourself. Why should anyone else honor you?

A client who had been feeling stuck in a dead-end job during a crossroads in his life used this exercise to recognize where he was not honoring all he was capable of doing. He was a truly gifted salesperson. He could develop a rapport with people immediately, no matter who they were and what they did. He had gotten used to being the top salesperson, regardless of which company he worked for. The problem was that he was selling gym memberships at swanky clubs. He hated the hours and the work environment. He felt unappreciated and knew that the next step up the ladder, managing the sales force, was not what he wanted to do. He wanted to make more money. He wanted more freedom, but he could not see his way to the next thing.

When we took a look at his professional strengths (closing a sale, organization, and time management) and his natural gifts (relationships, being an authoritative figure), we saw he was doing the right thing, but he was just in the wrong place. How could he capitalize on his strengths and make more money? The answer was simple: He needed a bigger-ticket item, and he needed to be around a different kind of people. He immediately thought of selling high-end real estate. In an expensive place like Manhattan, he could do very well.

At this writing he has completed his tests, he has his rental license, and he has made several thousand dollars in fees. His next goal is a broker's license. I have no doubt that his success will multiply. He didn't have to stretch far to find what would make him happy, but he did have to stop making excuses for not having what he wanted. He became unstuck by putting himself in a place where his gifts could work for him. He's now honoring them instead of using them to justify being unhappy. "I'm so talented, see how life stinks?" NO. Wrong. It doesn't stink; you just need to move yourself someplace where it smells better.

David did the same thing. He got out of a bad situation by not letting anyone or anything prevent him from letting his strengths come through. Once he had established an environment where that could happen, he was free to have a vision, and his direction for the future became clear. When he stopped putting up with the status quo, he came back to life. In fact, as we wrapped up our work together, he was talking about what he might do five years down the road when he had outgrown the new position he was about to assume.

You are what you tolerate!

Get Unstuck and Rev Up That Career

▼

1. Make a list of all the things you are procrastinating about or putting up with in your personal and professional life.
2. Eliminate EVERY item on that list.
3. Put extensive boundaries in place to keep those things from infringing on you again.
4. Get in touch with your strengths and gifts, and make the appropriate changes to honor them fully.
5. Make a pact with yourself never to put up with anything again.
6. Welcome back to living FULL-OUT!

THREE

On an Endless Treadmill. Burnout or Advancement— Which Will Come First?

"I work harder than anyone else I know. No one understands the pressure I'm under, and yet I have to admit, I'm not really sure where it's getting me."

A RE YOU CONSTANTLY APOLOGIZING FOR LETTING FAMILY AND friends down? Do you feel that no one can possibly understand how demanding it is to be as successful as you are? Are you pulled between the urge to slow down and the great feeling of being superhuman? Are you frustrated because no matter how much you put in, there is still a big gap between where you are and where you really want to be? No, this is not a commercial for a miracle energy pill, but a wake-up call. GET A LIFE! A real life. If you're running on a never-ending treadmill, you are not living a life; you're running a marathon, and you will burn out. Believe it or not, you will get much more of what you want if you get off the treadmill, take your eye off the road, and start looking at the sky. The farther up the ladder you want to climb, the more you'll need to be a visionary, not a crazed, overworked lunatic.

Admit it; the money's great. You don't know what else you would do, but to be honest, it's really not all that fun to be living the way you're living. The high is addictive, but it's really not that much fun, because your gift for high achievement contains your tragic flaw—you define your inherent value by how hard you work. You're not what you do; you're valuable because of who you are. If you can believe that, there is another way to be successful. Are you interested? It will mean making some major changes that won't seem logical at first, but if you are working this hard to get ahead, isn't it refreshing to know it can be painless and that you actually can do less, not more? This is possible if you're willing to go all the way. If you start judging this process right out of the gate, you'll run away as fast as you came to it, because it will threaten everything you ever thought you were. With that said, are you ready?

Britt was a thirty-nine-year-old vice president of sales for a major American pharmaceutical company when she first came to work with me. She was going a hundred miles an hour and was pumped on adrenaline, dealing with the effects of a reorganization in the company and managing her staff. She wanted to focus on giving her performance a tune-up as well as exploring the direction of her professional future. She very much wanted to be at a higher level, with more input into policy and major changes in her company.

In our first session, she reported that she had had a minor car accident recently because of her tendency to be rushing and doing a thousand things at once. She shared that she was always in high gear, with rarely a moment to spare. She took time for some leisure activities, like golf, but they were usually centered around business. She did not have any children, which gave her more time to be working constantly. She never accepted social invitations, and she admitted that everyone except her husband had just about given up on her. She sensed that she had to get off the treadmill, but she did not know how to do this, or what the benefit would really be.

It was clear that we needed to focus immediately on simplifying her life and on finding room to concentrate on what was truly necessary to get her ahead. Needless to say, she also needed to find time to have a life. We started where I start with most people, by clearing the slate. She was very willing to do some of the mundane "closet-cleaning" things I asked her to do, because she knew she had to get things in order to achieve some clarity. I knew she could only achieve mental space by making some physical space for it. She rearranged her physical space at home and at the office and recommitted to her fitness regime. Exercise helped her think more clearly, and having her physical space organized helped her feel more on top of things. She started to reduce her stress, and she began to understand what her priorities needed to be. She made more time to work *on* her job instead of just *in* it.

Britt's next step was to find time to nurture her relationships with her bosses and the managers under her. She had expressed her displeasure with having to accommodate a new boss who came with the merger her company had been through. I sensed a resentment starting there that was going to be an obstacle to her success. Her resentment came from her hurt pride and ego, and it was causing her to forget what would really make a difference in what she was trying to accomplish. In one of our conversations, I asked her to start finding ways to make her boss right instead of looking for where she could dwell on what he was doing wrong. At first, she thought I wasn't on her side, but I explained that I wasn't asking her to suck up to him. Instead, I wanted her to become his ally, in order to move the situation to a place she could live with. She recognized the value in making a more positive choice, and decided to be devoted 100 percent to supporting her boss's success.

In initiating an opportunity to have a better relationship with her boss, Britt spent more time with him in person and via e-mail, which she would not have done otherwise. They got along well. She had no idea what an impact this had until her new boss, only seven weeks later, recommended her for a position two or three levels above where she was. On her fortieth birthday she was offered the position of national director of sales operations for the company. She would now report directly to the president of the company. This was amazingly exciting for her but also dangerous, because her workaholic tendencies were being called on again in full force.

We are now working on developing Britt to be the leader and visionary she has always known she can be; there is no reason that she can't get closer to the top of this organization or be a CEO. We are working to have her learn how to do less and achieve more. The projects she takes on are bigger, but we want to shift her from being a doer to being a leader. As she moves up the ladder, it means less doing and more being still, so she can anticipate what is next for the marketplace and for the company. She is finally working on the policies and issues that she has always wanted to have an impact on. She now takes the time to build strong relationships within the company. In addition, as she becomes more and more committed to balancing her life and giving herself more space, her world has responded by giving her greater leadership responsibility. She's not getting busier, but becoming clearer. At this writing, there is more change in her company, and she is being considered for an even greater leadership role.

What would you think if I told you you were an addict? Yup, a junkie. You are. You are addicted to your own adrenaline. It's how you get through the day, isn't it? Do you go full throttle and then collapse at the end of the day? You think it's because life is so hectic, but it's really because you are using adrenaline as your fuel source. Adrenaline tells you you're great; it gives you superhuman power. You probably like it, but, sorry, it's not sustainable. You're going to need a much more reliable and healthy fuel source if you want to get off the treadmill and get what you truly want. You might choose peace, creativity, passion, or vision. Now, don't run off just yet. I know it sounds lofty, but I bet it sounds appealing, even if it doesn't seem possible to you yet.

This whole adrenaline issue is a by-product of today's lifestyle. We live in an adrenaline-driven society. It's a tall order —to step away from the sweeping rush of being in a world that operates on adrenaline—but once you can get in touch with finding your own natural pace, you won't want to go back. You will learn to work smarter and to remain effective in a world that is going a hundred miles an hour. You will stop being in crisis mode, and you will excel without rushing. Are you ready to take the first step?

Eliminate whatever triggers your adrenaline. There are probably certain circumstances and activities that get the adrenaline pumping. Your job is to identify what they are and then eliminate the triggers completely, eliminating the adrenaline rushes. Possible triggers may be caffeine, office or home drama, gossip, deadlines, phone interruptions, rushing, or the high of a big win. You'll need to get to the source of each one and erase it so it can't come back to bite you. For example, if caffeine sets you off, stop drinking it. If drama gets your juices going, refuse to get hooked by it. If phone interruptions make you crazy, don't take every call. Let your assistants take messages, and return all of them during one block of time. If you get a rush from a big win, be aware when adrenaline is kicking in, and find another way to celebrate.

Once you start getting the adrenaline habit kicked, you should start feeling more at ease and be able to see things more clearly than you could before. The crises have probably started to decrease, and now you have the distance to see what the usual sources of the crises were and what you may need to do to address them. You'll probably need to simplify and mainstream systems, train people who are not up to speed or let them go. You've gotten to the source of your adrenaline triggers; now get to the source of the other problems you face.

This might be a lot to ask. Problems are as addictive as adrenaline. It makes sense; the bigger your paycheck, the bigger the size of the problems you solve. Your whole value may be attached to problems. If you like being a hero, problems may be your friends. Many of us get energy from having problems, but you can do better. This is the next step in becoming the leader you want to be. To stop having problems, get to the source of each one and make sure you take care of it so well that it can't ever come back to bite you. If this is the first time anyone's ever suggested this to you, it probably sounds impossible.

You'll need to make a shift in perception to stop having problems. Instead of facing problems as your adversaries and ultimately defining yourself and measuring your worth by your ability to solve them, look at problems from the other side: A problem is an opportunity to design a system to permanently eliminate that problem. Let your success be determined by how bored you become when you have no more problems to solve.

You'll have to keep others from bringing their problems to you too. Until now you've probably been inviting problems to your doorstep. "But it's my job to deal with other peoples' concerns." I know, I know. You can train them, however, to do some thinking before they bring the problem to your door. Many of my clients sport a sign on their door or desk that says: PROBLEM-FREE ZONE—ONLY SOLUTIONS MAY ENTER! This shields them from becoming a dumping ground. People must come in with part of a solution before my clients consent to discuss the problem. You'll need to do the same. We talked about boundaries in chapter 2; this is another way of creating and enforcing a boundary. Things will still happen, but if you're off adrenaline and shielding yourself from problems, you will be well on your way to reducing your stress and getting off the treadmill. As in Britt's case, the treadmill keeps you on an endless chase, but ironically, the chase is taking you *away* from what you want.

Being a workaholic and deriving your value from how much you can rush through in a day and how many problems you can solve go hand in hand. If you can come to define yourself by *who* you are and not *what* you do, you'll be able to master your addictions to adrenaline and problems, and you'll be able to step off the treadmill for good. You'll establish a higher quality of life, and you'll have the room to be the kind of leader you want to be.

*　　*　　*

Marie had been a top salesperson for one of the big telecommunications companies for years. She made great money, and got all the recognition she could ever want, but she was on a crash course to permanent burnout. She was one of the most driven people I had ever worked with, and yet when we discussed being an adrenaline junkie and stepping off the treadmill, she realized she didn't have the energy to buck the system all the way. She would be a trout swimming upstream trying to implement steps to balance her life in an environment that couldn't support it. As hard as it was on her ego to give up the limelight, she went ahead full throttle to the next level to become management. She also knew that being a manager in sales would not give her her life back, so she applied for a marketing position in another branch of her company. We reworked her résumé and prepared her to make a good case for herself, and she got the job. She earns the same as she did before, but she works fewer hours. As she puts it, "I finally have time to do all the things I love—be with my husband and my family, exercise, and enjoy life." She no longer defines herself by her achievements. She discovered what makes her happy, pursued that, and remained highly successful. She has lost nothing. She has gained time, pleasure, and fulfillment.

Ask yourself why you've been running so hard, anyway. What are you running from? Unfortunately for some people, this is where they find out they've been avoiding facing a bad marriage or the emptiness that would be waiting at home if they weren't consuming themselves with work. Others are clinging to an old work ethic that says if you're not suffering, you're not succeeding. Britt and Marie learned to attain their worth from something other than their busyness, and they were highly motivated to recapture their lives and to pursue what they really wanted. Let's assume you want that too and keep moving forward. We're making way for great things to happen here.

The next step in shedding your constant overwhelming and workaholic-on-a-treadmill tendencies will be valuing other people and including them in your success. "But I do that," you say. If you have recognized yourself in this chapter, you value people for the results they can bring you and not much more. I hear you protesting, but keep reading. If you've been running as fast as I think you've been, you haven't had time to pay attention long enough to have an impact on anyone. You've needed them to accomplish a result, and that's it.

To get the most from people and feel supported by them as well, you'll need to give a lot more than you've been doing. The true measure of how you are doing as a leader is not the number of followers you have; it is the number of leaders you have developed around you. When you can turn this around for yourself, you will start seeing amazing things happen for you. Refocus your intent, and start looking at people differently. They will respond to you in a new way. You won't find it hard to maneuver your way through your day-to-day activities. People will cooperate with you as they never have before. When you were an adrenalized problem addict, they avoided getting in your path, or only brought you problems. Now they will relate to you on much more interesting and productive levels. You'll have more support than you need, and you will be off the treadmill completely. Here's what you have to do to start feeling this change:

1) **Start acknowledging people.** You probably already do this to a degree, but you want to go even deeper. Most people give

compliments: "I thought that was a great presentation." "Good work on that campaign." "I liked what you had to say in there." Acknowledging someone would sound like this: "You have a great sense of how to engage a group of people." "Your tenacity made this happen for us." "Your perception is keen." Can you see the difference?

The first batch of compliments were really about you and *your* opinion. In the second, you were telling the people who *they* are. That's about them, and they love it. Wouldn't you? You are reflecting something about them that they are glad to hear. When you start becoming that kind of supporter of people, they want to support you right back.

2) Develop people. Acknowledging is one way to do this. When people see themselves in how you describe them, they grow on the spot. They fill up the space you generously make for them, and they want to do more. To develop others, you'll need to start bringing out the best in them. Stop focusing solely on results, and start bringing their latency into fulfillment. Ask a lot of them. I don't mean that you should dump on them or give them unrealistic deadlines or expectations, but rather that you should ask more of them than they would of themselves, simply because you recognize their potential. People see in themselves what we see in them. The bigger the vision, the bigger their willingness to use and display the potential you have shown them.

One caution: This is very powerful. Do not use it as a weapon. You have to be genuine; it will backfire on you if you are not. Do not use it as a manipulative tool to get what you want. Leadership is a gift and a responsibility. It also carries potential power to damage. Use it carefully.

3) Guide them to their strengths. Just as you're reading this book to bring out the best in yourself, use what you know to guide others to their best. Tell the truth. Help people see where they are cheating themselves and where they can do better. Somewhere in your past, someone told you the truth about where you were great and where you needed work, and although it may have been hard to hear, you'd thank them for it today. Be that for someone else. Coach them!

4) Allow people to manage up. Let them tell you how to help them do a great job. It may mean listening to what *you* can do better. Your ego can take it. If it can't, you may need more help than I can give you. Give people the room to give you advice, and you'll start having more productive people. They won't be operating from the external expectations that you've put on them, but rather from a plan tailor-made for them, by them. They will perform better, just as all humans do better when they are allowed to find their own way, and they'll have your support in doing so. You can't do it alone, so you can't afford not to do this. If you've been a power monster, always needing to be right, now is the time to give it up, cold turkey. Do it.

Let's review:

1. You've broken your adrenaline addiction.
2. You've stopped getting your identity from solving problems.
3. You've recognized the high-yield return on the investment of nurturing an environment of leaders.

Britt went through these three stages in a matter of weeks. It could take you several months or longer, but if you're truly committed to being the leader you know you can be, this should not stop you—that is, of course, assuming that you want a greater leadership role. If you just wanted to get off the treadmill and are now satisfied with where you are, there is no need to read the rest of this chapter. You should be experiencing a richer work and home life. Congratulations! If, however, you have aspirations for greater leadership, the next three areas will be crucial. We are headed toward freeing you up further than getting off the treadmill allowed. Leadership comes from vision, and when you were bogged down in detail and burnt out, there was no room for vision. Vision has to find you; you can't force it. The following sections should prepare you to meet up with it.

INTEGRITY

Integrity is a strong word. If I questioned your integrity, you would probably get defensive with me. That's probably because you think of integrity as an adherence to a code of values. This is what the American Heritage dictionary says integrity is. The dictionary also carries a second definition of it, which is the one I will allude to often in this section. It says: "soundness, completeness, unity." An architectural structure needs integrity to stand tall and last long. So do you. When a support pillar is cracked, the structure has no integrity; when it is sound, it has integrity. We will be looking to see if your working self has integrity.

Integrity is different for everyone, so it is hard to pinpoint. I would venture to guess that if I told you to take the high road in every situation, you would know exactly what I was talking about. The way I see it, that is what integrity is: not compromising yourself, and taking the high road whenever you can.

You don't tell little lies to yourself to feel better when you know you have abandoned yourself and what you stand for; you do what you know is right—not necessarily by someone else's code of ethics, but rather by your own. It's really very simple. So why is it so hard? Because we are afraid of the consequences.

Well, you'll just have to become fearless if you want to step into that greater leadership role. You'll have to take risks, and your integrity will become crucial as your criteria for taking those risks. The greater your attention to the wholeness that will keep you and your organization afloat, the closer you are to reaching it. If you haven't been promoted to where you think you need to be, stop here and take a good, hard look: Your integrity is not as strong as it needs to be. Find that place. When are you not telling the truth to yourself or somebody else? When have you not kept your word to yourself or to somebody else? Be harsh about what the truth is; white lies aren't acceptable here. Every flaw in your integrity is robbing you of the energy you need to get to where you want to go, so you'd better clean it up before it washes you out.

Your integrity can be compromised in blatant or subtle ways. For example, in working with the head of an organization, we came across a subtle breach in his integrity that was costing him dearly with his staff, and he didn't even realize it until it was almost too late. He told me that many of the people on his staff were being very cautious around him. They seemed to be avoiding him and keeping away from discussing major issues. He couldn't understand why. Together, we tried to uncover the source of this.

In passing, he mentioned that he didn't think his staff understood his humor. I asked him why he thought that was. He said he would make jokes at meetings, and no one seemed to find them funny. AH! Bingo! We found it! "Were these jokes about people who weren't there? Were they somewhat derogatory in nature?" I asked. "Yes," he said, "but I didn't mean anything by them." He may not have meant anything by them, but he made every person in that room feel unsafe. Of course they avoided contact with him; they were afraid they would be the brunt of his next joke. It was hard for him to accept that what he thought was harmless banter was actually destructive, but when he saw the breach in integrity, he took the high road, and he brought trust back to order.

Integrity Check-in

Write down ten places where your integrity is less than ideal with yourself or with somebody else. It could be a subtle breach or a big one. If you are uncomfortable around someone else, or have a nagging issue concerning yourself, it's a place to stop and check for a breach. For example, if you were into adrenaline and problems before, you were out of integrity with yourself. You were causing yourself undue stress and doing damage.

Once you have targeted these ten places, take radical action to make them whole again. Clean up every one of them. You may need to have a few heart-to-hearts if these are breaches against other people. Turn this around, and you'll be able to go on to the next step on your leadership track.

Britt had been allowing several of her staff members to come into her office and gossip and complain about another staff member who was not the ideal co-worker. She had allowed this, and she contributed to it by showing her empathy and adding a comment or two of her own. When we discussed it, she realized that she wasn't on the high road; she knew she shouldn't be having these conversations behind this guy's back. The next time it happened, she said, "I can no longer talk about anyone who is not in the room. Should we call him in so we can all talk about this together?" People were appalled. Of course, they didn't have the guts to face this guy, or they would have done so already. Britt's new stand actually stopped the malicious gossiping altogether.

RESPONSIBILITY

Taking the high road is also going to include taking responsibility. Don't get me wrong; I know you're responsible, or you wouldn't be where you are today. What I'm talking about is the next level of taking responsibility. You've already conquered problems on one level, and this is the next one. Taking responsibility doesn't mean burdening yourself with the weight of the world, your company, or your division; that is how you got burnt out in the first place. Rather, it means leading people out of a problem and blame mentality and into being solution oriented. In other words, don't take responsibility for the problem, but do take responsibility for its solution. That has "leader" written all over it. That is what you want, isn't it? So what is going to change? What do you have to do to become that person?

Maybe an example will help: A breakdown in communication in an HR department where my client, Mike, was the VP was big enough to cause some semidisastrous consequences, including putting a couple of jobs in jeopardy. Fingers were being pointed, and people were really out of sorts. Before it got too ugly, Mike called a meeting and declared that he was taking responsibility for the whole situation. People reacted as if he were a lamb going to slaughter. They tried to save him from some perceived awful fate. They said things like "You can't be blamed for this. You had nothing to do with it." He explained that it wasn't about taking the blame, but about taking responsibility; in other words, finding a way for everyone to win. He felt that he was as responsible as everyone else. It was his department; he was on-premises, with the job of reporting directly to the president, so he should have had his finger on the pulse of what went on. People were stunned, but they stopped their bickering and were ready to find a solution. They rallied behind Mike and were ready to get past this mishap and on to solutions that would save everyone's job.

The leader knows how to get people to make these shifts. The leader doesn't have to be perfect, but rather needs the clarity to see where to step in and shift the focus and energy to something productive. If you were still on a treadmill, you would not be able to do this.

INTUITION

I'm sure you've heard that scientists say we only use a very small percentage of our brain's capacity. Underusing our intuition contributes to this. I'm going to reintroduce you to a skill that is going to help change that. That skill is using your intuition. Intuition is underrated. Women tend to be better at it than men, but the top CEOs and executives, male or female, know it is what their best decisions are made of. Intuition is more than a hunch, and yet cannot necessarily be linked to logic. It is a powerful knowledge that cannot be denied. It is in everyone, but it is only available to those who are willing to hear it. Every step in this chapter has helped to get you ready to tap into this. The noise of clutter, disorganization, adrenaline, breaches of integrity, and bailing out on yourself was keeping you from it. If you haven't relied on intuition before, now is the time. It's not hard to do, but it will take commitment to develop this latent quality. What awaits you is the opportunity to shorten the time it takes to make decisions, to stay ahead of yourself, and to trust yourself to a greater degree.

The Three Keys to Developing Your Intuition

There are three key ingredients you will need to incorporate to bring the benefits of your intuition to light. The first one is finding time for creative silence each and every day. Take at least fifteen minutes a day to be in complete silence—no interruptions, no distractions. It doesn't matter if you do this at home or at the office. You don't need to do anything during this time. It can run the gamut, from just staring out the window for fifteen minutes, to meditating during that time. If you can do more than fifteen minutes, then by all means, please do. The point is to take the time. The earth may not move, nor may you have any great revelations, but I can guarantee that you will start feeling a cumulative effect of taking this time. You will start feeling clearer, responding to things with a sense of ease instead of reacting to things that get you ruffled. You will get answers to questions you've been pondering at the most unusual times. You won't need the same kind of time you once needed to accomplish the same tasks. I noticed how well this worked for me;

it would take me hours to get through work on days that I didn't take creative silence, and then I would get through a similar workload in an hour on days that I did.

The second ingredient you need to use your intuition consistently is to know how to frame your questions or concerns. The way you phrase the question is everything. If it is too subjective, you will not be able to interpret what your intuition sends you. For example, "Should we go ahead with the merger?" may be too vague to help you. If you ask, "What do I need to know about going ahead with this merger?" or "What issues do I need to evaluate in hiring this person?" you are more likely to access concrete useful information. Avoid questions that sound like you're looking into a crystal ball, like "Will I get a raise?" Yes, you will get a raise sometime in your lifetime, although it may be ten years from now. You need to be specific in order to use your intuition well. Being specific will make all the difference here and with many other aspects of being a leader. Too many people are afraid to be wrong or to rule out other possibilities by narrowing the field. Your decisiveness is essential in this case, and it won't hurt to develop it anyway.

For example, a client who headed a regional sales team was intrigued but dubious when I asked him to start taking fifteen minutes a day for creative silence. By our next appointment the following week, he had managed to fit it in a couple of times, with impressive results. He had been trying to fill a position in his department for months, and never had more than one candidate at any given time. He was frustrated, so he felt he had nothing to lose by trying my unusual request. After taking his fifteen minutes one morning and asking himself what he needed to know about finding a candidate, he went about business as usual, but he kept thinking about an old boss of his all day, until he realized that his intuition might be trying to tell him something. He decided to give his old boss a call. During the course of the conversation, he mentioned that he had been trying to fill a position. The conversation yielded three candidates for the job. He wrote it off as coincidence, but only after telling me that it had happened and remarking how interesting the coincidence was. I don't believe in coincidences; his creative silence yielded more results than any of his fruitless searching.

The third ingredient is learning how to distinguish intuition from fear. You may have pictured a haunting image in your mind of something bad happening that you perceived as an omen of doom. Chances are you turned out to be wrong. Anything loud, jarring, frightening, or upsetting is more likely to be fear than intuition. If your intuition needs to send you a warning, it will do so in a gentle way. Instead of getting a picture in your mind of stepping off the curb to meet with a grim destiny, you're more likely to get the feeling you should look over your shoulder at the corner before you take a step. As a large truck whisks by, you'll probably say, "Something told me to take one more look." Intuition will always be gentle. That is how you will know it from fear.

A high-level executive client of mine thought I was crazy when I asked him to start taking creative silent time every day. He laughed, but he was intrigued enough to do it. Well, he didn't doubt me for long. A month after he started building in this time, which he usually took in his office, he had a strong intuitive feeling that he needed to cancel a multimillion-dollar project that he had been working on for months. He could not back up his intuitive feeling with logic. He had already gone so far with convincing all the right people to put the money up for it, and he had rallied very hard to gain consensus. Throwing it all away would not make sense from a logical standpoint, but he knew it was right to do so. At the risk of confusing a lot of people, he canceled the project, just before he was to pay out $10 million in start-up fees. It was a good thing that money never went out; within weeks of the cancellation, the company he had been negotiating with was closed down, and the owners were arrested for tax evasion. All their company assets were frozen, and liens were put on all their accounts. My client's money would have been gone or tied up for a very long time, and the project would have been derailed. My client doesn't laugh at what I ask him to do anymore.

Everyone has latent intuition, and it is the kind of self-trust and foresight that the leader you say you want to be must have. It's not an exact science, but the more you use it, the easier it will become to rely on it.

VISION

Vision, vision, vision. No leader leaves home without it. Why would you? How could you, if you say you want to be at the very top of your organization? You can't have cooperation from other people if they don't trust that you have a vision for where you want them to go. It is your job to carry the vision for them all and to make it so compelling that people are propelled to take action to get there. This will be your job. This is what every gifted leader has.

A vision is a compelling image of an achievable future. It is grand in scope, and it may seem improbable if you try to make it come to reality right this minute, but it is achievable. It should be bigger than you or bigger than your company. Having a vision of living in a huge home and making a lot of money is inspiring to some, but it is ultimately only going to matter to you and to others who will benefit from it. A vision has to be bigger than you to merit others' being pulled to it, which means that it has to be for a good greater than your own personal benefit. For example, my vision is that everyone can love what they do and lead amazing lives. To that end, my mission is to coach as many people as I can to get there and to create systems by which people can make that possible. Sure, I have goals and desires in my personal and professional life, but the real motivator that keeps me going is the vision I passionately believe is possible.

I once worked with a three-partner firm to create its vision and mission statement. The partners started off thinking the way most people do, trying to come up with a vision of what they would look like in five years. Vision is bigger than that; theirs had to be bigger than their business plan. It had to be the reason they existed as a business (besides creating wealth, of course). By the end of the day, they had their vision, and they were fired up (a sure sign that you've hit on an authentic vision for you or your company). Their vision was to be the company that changed the way their entire industry did business. They felt they were the good guys in an industry in which many found it easy to cheat the customer. It gave them a great sense of purpose to reorient their actions around this vision. It was powerful, compelling—not easy, but achievable. From there, we created the mission to support that vision.

What is your company's vision statement? Go out and do research about other companies and how they express their vision. Get familiar with this, yet know that the vision is not going to be created by one person. Everyone has to buy in and touch it; just get familiar to try it on for size. Having your own vision is more important.

Now sit down and figure out your personal vision. What do you care about? What's bigger than you that you can accomplish with your exact skills and talents? Leaders see something that not everyone else can, but others are compelled because they can communicate it in a way that makes it seem possible. You will need to know how to access this if you really want to be at the top the way you say you do.

Being a leader starts at home with you. It's what you see, and what you make your life about, that fuels you to be out in front. You don't have to wait for anyone to name you a leader. Just start being it for yourself, and see what follows suit. A vision can't be forced, so if it becomes a chore and doesn't come to you easily, let it go for now. Focus on taking care of other parts of your life first. Take responsibility, clear up any breaches in your integrity, mend or nurture existing relationships, and do a little life cleanup. It may help make your vision clearer.

Your Personal Vision

1. Imagine what is possible that you can make a great contribution to. Don't be afraid to make it very, very big. Accomplishing the vision just has to be possible, not necessarily immediately probable.
2. Think about what you can do to make that vision come true. This becomes your mission.
3. What action do you need to take to fulfill the mission? That action will shape your sense of purpose and accentuate where you are gifted as a leader.

Increasing your leadership role in an organization should not mean taking on more than you can bear. It means increasing your scope and vision until you can effect the greatest change. I hope you've adopted some new insights and tools for stopping the workaholic treadmill and stepping into true leadership. You should be more comfortable about enlarging your role by doing less. You no longer need to have problems and a myriad of tasks to feel that you are in charge. Also, keep in mind that being a leader doesn't limit your choices at all to being at the top of the executive line or waiting for that opportunity. It can start now, but you'll need your presence of mind and a lot of physical and emotional space to fill that role. Step off the treadmill, and really be here.

Stop running and start leading.

Get off the Treadmill and on the Leadership Track

▼

1. Get off adrenaline.
2. Give up having problems.
3. Start investing in other people.
4. Clean up your integrity.
5. Take responsibility.
6. Develop your intuition.
7. Tap into your vision.
8. Become the leader you are, NOW.

FOUR

Having It All, but Really Wanting Something Else

"It's too late to make a change now. How can I walk away from everything I've built?"

ROBERT WAS THE OWNER OF A SUCCESSFUL INSURANCE FIRM. HE hired me as his coach because he felt pulled in so many directions that he did not feel he was being as effective as he could be in any of them. Part of what made his life so busy was that he valued teaching and inspiring other people, and he always did so in his day-to-day affairs. It was how he would prefer to spend his time. This made him popular with his clients, but his business was suffering because he spent so much time away from it. He was also very devoted to his family, and had high expectations of himself as a participatory husband and parent. To the outside, he looked like a man who had it all, but on the inside he was torn and wanted to do more of what he loved without risking his financial security.

With a year of hard work, he put all the pieces in place to have a strong business that could run without him. He hired and trained new staff, delegated some tasks, and reorganized the way things were done so that he was free to go after the sizable accounts that only he could close. He tightened up the financial aspects of the business as well. Revenues increased by about 30 percent, and his stress went down significantly. He now had a lot more time to spend with his family. Once all this was taken care of, it was time to add more of what he loved most to the picture. Now he had time to teach and inspire others without having it cost him. As we wrapped up our work together, he was finding opportunities to teach, train, and speak on sales and motivational topics to other insurance and sales professionals. It was a chance not only to increase his income, but to do more of the things he really cared about.

Rachel was a VP with a major New York City public relations firm. She had worked for eleven years to get to where she was in a cutthroat, fast-paced business. It was glamorous, it was exciting, and it was everything she thought she ever wanted. When she found herself unhappy, overworked, and uninspired, she was dumbfounded by the irony of it all. Was this what she had worked for all these years?

Rachel hired me when she knew she could no longer ignore her feeling that she had to do something, although she wasn't sure what she wanted to do. It was hard to decide to leave something she had been building for eleven years, but she didn't see any other choice. We narrowed down her ideas about what she might do to a few that she was fascinated with. Before she made any decisions about leaving where she was, I asked her to find out as much as she could about the three new fields she most wanted to be in. After having done research on all of them, she chose the one that she had the strongest attraction to. It was light-years away from where she was now, but she knew she had to do it. She wanted to work in a healing profession—specifically, doing therapy that included working with dolphins. She had had an experience swimming with dolphins that she had never forgotten and ever since had been drawn to doing more with them. It would mean training and moving to Florida, and she had her marriage and her husband's career to consider.

The next step was to brainstorm all the possible paths that could get her from where she was now to where she wanted to be. Rachel's biggest personal challenge was giving up her very ample income, but she knew if that was all that was keeping her at the firm, it wasn't worth her sanity. After much consideration, she decided to set up shop at home, providing PR and writing services. She and her husband moved to reduce their expenses by getting out of Manhattan. Soon after the move, there was an unexpected surprise. Her husband got a huge promotion, which they decided would become extra savings. She has started plans to go to Florida to train a few times a year with the dolphins. Her husband has his own dream of starting a surf shop in Florida, and they are now in the process of planning their big move. It may take them a couple years to make the transition, but she is so happy now that she can be patient and carefully plan how to make the rest of the dream come true.

Successful, but unhappy. Hmmmmm. Something is wrong with that picture. It's not uncommon for people to find themselves in what looks to the rest of the world like a great place, but leaves them feeling edgy, bored, unsatisfied, or plain miserable leading a life they're supposed to be loving. It is actually very simple: internals vs. externals. Are you living your life according to external prompts from society, the media, old messages from childhood, and your own "shoulds," or are you living the life of your dreams, prompted by what makes you tick from the inside? If you're unhappy, it's the former.

I've seen this too many times to ignore it: People make decisions about their lives that really have nothing to do with themselves, but are rather a reflection of external expectations put upon them. Take a moment to ask yourself this question: "Why am I doing what I am doing?" Did you decide at twenty-two that you were nobody if you didn't make it in the big city, and then wake up fifteen years later wondering why? Did you get a job right out of school and stick with the same company because that was what you were supposed to do? Did you become an executive just to prove to someone that you could do it?

I went to college because that's what was expected of me at eighteen, when I really knew in my heart that I wanted some time to decide what I wanted to study in college before going. If your choices were based on someone else's opinions, they were made in response to *external* expectations. If they really came from you, it was an *internal* choice, and you're probably not in dire straits and wanting to do something else. If you're at the mercy of externals, you've probably ignored what you really want to do for a long time because of everything you *have* to do or *should* do. By now you're pretty numb to it, except that you're not happy. You've stayed too long at the fair, my friend. You've ignored yourself again because it seemed impossible to do anything about it.

Oh, don't say it. I can hear it from here: "Well, yeah, if I didn't have a mortgage to pay and college tuition to save for, maybe I could do something for me." I hear this all the time, but surprisingly it is not from the people I coach. Those ready to do something about it don't wallow in this. Those that think there is nothing they can do, coaching or no coaching, are the ones that complain and wallow in it. Fear and trepidation are normal; blind defeat is a nail in the coffin. You're right; there is nothing you can do—not because of the circumstances, but because you're not willing to have it work any other way. "There are other people to consider besides me." You're absolutely right, and those people would probably be so happy if you were doing something that made you happy.

Let's be practical; I'm not talking about running off and escaping it all. We're looking at making changes that will include what will make you happy and maintain your priorities. Just bring yourself to the top of those priorities, and this won't seem so impossible. Believe me, your kids will be better off in the long run having had a fulfilled, attentive parent than full tuition, gratis. You've fallen into the lifestyle trap. The money's been good, you contribute to a good life for your family, you've invested years in this path, but don't forget, you're not happy. Don't be married to this lifestyle. You can create a different one. You deserve to like what you do. You deserve to LOVE what you do. To start living from internals, you are going to have to put yourself first and make a lot of changes. I am asking you to put yourself first, and become very, very selfish. Not greedy selfish; good selfish—putting yourself first in the name of your happiness in a way that will not hurt anyone else.

I recently worked with a senior magazine editor named Dean who thought he was ready to make a career change. We worked together on several paths that he could take to other fields of interest. He started to pursue them, but no solid opportunities presented themselves. As we evaluated each option, I encouraged Dean to become more and more selfish. I asked him to stop focusing on what he thought he *could* have, and to start focusing on what he *wanted*. The more committed he became to honoring what he wanted, the more opportunities seemed to arise. The greatest opportunity came from within his current publishing company—there was a sudden reorganization.

By now, it had become clear that Dean didn't necessarily need to change careers; he had just needed to understand clearly what he really needed to be happy at his job. He met with the publishers and made specific requests about the kinds of topics he wanted to write about, the people he wanted to work with, and where and how he wanted to contribute. They gave him all of it, and a raise to boot. There now are other possibilities available to him later on if he decides he can do even better. The bottom line was not being afraid to be selfish and flat-out asking for what he wanted.

I'm going to ask you a couple of simple questions. I want you to take a deep breath and answer truthfully from the deepest place you can reach. Here's the first question: "If you were making half the money you are making now, would you still want to do what you are doing?" If your answer is no, go on to the next question: "What do you want?" Really, truly, unrealistic as it may sound: "What do you want?" Whatever your answer, it should ring through you as the greatest truth you've ever told. Now let's see what we can do about it.

One way to know whether what you want is a pipe dream or connected to something very real for you is to check it against your values. Your values express you at your core. If you've been longing to do something else, that very thing is probably a value waiting to be expressed. Values, in this context, are not about your ethics and morals, but about what you are naturally attracted to doing and being. These are the internals that we were talking about. When you are expressing your values, you are most fulfilled. Your values are what call you, whether or not you can make money at it. Add making money at it, and we've hit nirvana.

Values are organic sources of success that are already in you. To reorient your life around them will allow you to eliminate some of the high cost many people pay for trying to "make it." When you are expressing your values and getting paid for it, you are succeeding at no emotional cost to you. There is no trade-off or sacrifice; work doesn't feel like work. In fact, work becomes you. Values make it possible for you to be expressing your greatest talents with the most ease, and where a sense of purpose can't help but prevail. They are not very hard to uncover if you're not 100 percent sure of what yours are.

Values: Your Keys to Organic Success

1. Think about what you love to do professionally and personally.
2. Think about the most significant or meaningful personal and professional accomplishments in your life.
3. Think about things you loved to do as a kid or young adult that you have gotten away from now.
4. Think about who you naturally are to other people personally and professionally. Are you a teacher? Motivator? Nurturer? Leader? Adventurer? Follower?
5. What are the qualities you need to express in yourself or your life to feel happy?
6. Write all these things down.

Take a look at each of the events or activities that you have written down. Now focus on them, and ask yourself what values are expressed by them. Look for words that would symbolize what went on there. For example: If you used to paint in high school and college, what values got expressed there? It may have been beauty or creativity. You value beauty and creativity. Other values may be teaching, freedom, spirituality, inspiring, excellence, community, influencing others, relating, leading, discovering, adventure, risk. Look at the essence of each activity, and you'll find the essence of who you are. You'll find your values.

Once you've written them all down, pick the top three. Measure them against each other; decide which are really essentially you. Don't choose what you think you should value. Don't choose what you want to value. Only choose those that are truly a value for you. The most precious one of those three expresses your deepest value. That top value just may be your whole raison d'être. Dramatic, huh? You have to admit, it's pretty exciting.

Great. So, you've got that figured out. Now what? Now comes figuring out how to reorient around what you've found out. You can't ignore it anymore. Once you know what your values are, you have no excuse to let the status quo keep eating you up. Reorienting around your values may mean crossing over to a whole new line of work altogether, but don't let that scare you. Once you have a plan to make such a crossover, you'll start feeling even better. The plan is everything.

THE CROSSOVER PLAN

The biggest things that will determine what your plan looks like are time and money. Are you in the position, like Rachel, to cut back and live on less income to make your transition, or will you be more in Robert's position of refocusing your efforts, but staying where you are in terms of employment? That is the first decision you have to make. The second thing you want to decide is when you would like to complete this transition. If it's tomorrow or five years from now, this will make a big difference in your plan.

Even though you have determined your values in the last exercise, maybe you're still not sure what direction you might like to head in. Let's take a side trip for a moment if this applies to you. Take a stab at three possible jobs or industries that you would like to be involved in. There can be more than three, but you cannot focus on more than three at any given time. You have to eliminate one before you can add another. When you have the three, start making a list of all the people you know who may know those industries or may know someone in those areas. Talk to three people a day who can help you get a better idea of how you fit those areas or what you would have to do to be marketable in them. Three people a day times five days a week is fifteen people a week. Don't let anyone off the phone until you have the names of two more people to speak to. Once you've done your research, you should have a better idea of where you'd like to be going next. Get cracking. I didn't say it was going to be easy, but it will be fun knowing you're on the way to something new.

We're back from the side trip; this is where you pick up as everyone else would. Once you know your crossover goal, it's time to come up with every possible way that can get you there. Sit down with five different people at different times and, one by one, have them brainstorm with you how to get from here to there. Approach each meeting as if you had not had any others.

For the sake of these conversations, every idea is a great idea. You cannot say no to any of it. Anything is possible. Go from the sublime to the ridiculous. When you have five different possible paths for making your crossover, come up with one master plan that you intend to try first. It can be a complete version from one of your brainstorming sessions, or it can be one that you compiled from different pieces of each session. If you are visual, you may want to map out the plan as a drawing or chart. Whatever the case, the one that appeals to you the most is the one you will start with. Congratulations; you now have your plan.

Putting It into Action

Making a change like this can require the attention of a full-time job. Chances are, it won't be an overnight transition, so you'll need to set up a structure that will support you. In Robert's case it took a year to reorganize his business so he could do what he most wanted to do. Get as many people involved in this crossover as you can. Have more support than you need. Delegate pieces of the plan, and engage as many cheerleaders as you can find. You're going to need them.

Pick a time once a week to sit down for an hour and focus on your plan. Choose it now. There is no wriggling away on this. Wednesday night? From five to six o'clock? Great. This is your strategic time. Measure what you've done and what you're going to need to do. Put your plan on a time line. Use this check-in time to make sure you're on track. Count on needing five to ten hours a week to execute your plan. Whatever you do, the weekly check-in time is critical. It will keep you focused on going for what you say you want, and it will keep you from getting swallowed up by everyday life.

There is also a cumulative benefit to visiting your new plan every week. Not only are you taking action toward achieving it, but you will find that the mental attention to it starts drawing your new future to you much more quickly. Sound magical? Maybe it is, but I can vouch for it, having seen it work with hundreds of people. For example, I recently completed an eighteen-month coaching relationship with a client who had done tremendously well with me. (You'll hear her story later.) We spent most of the time taking action on her work-related goals, but we talked about all of her goals often. Some of her personal goals were to join the board of an artistic nonprofit organization, to start a garden, and to see amazing places in the world. She read her goals list every week before our call.

Within a few weeks of our final conversation, she had achieved all of them. She now sits on the board of a theater in New York City, she is buying a home that will finally mean she'll have her own garden, and a friend has asked her to come along on an overseas adventure. How's that for attracting what you want? Do you get the message? Focus, focus, focus.

Here is another scenario in which focus, action, and persistence paid off: Joyce was a brilliant Asian woman with several Ivy League degrees whose success in international banking was a great source of pride to her family. Her career closely mirrored her father's, and she came to me to help her find her next move in the banking field. It did not take long to see that she had no passion for her work. She had based her whole career on externals and on others' expectations. After much prodding, she admitted that she had a secret ambition to someday design her own line of clothes and have a fashion empire. Once the secret was out, she had no other choice but to pursue it. Joyce now had the arduous task of breaking into a field in which she had no experience.

In evaluating what she did have that was transferable, she decided that her international and financial background could be an entrée into the field. She could learn the business side of the fashion business and develop her design skills from there. It took almost a year of networking, informational interviews, and self-education before Joyce started to be considered a serious candidate for a position. She even flew overseas to study the marketplace and meet some people in the business in order to get up to speed. There were many rejections, but with each one she learned something new. Finally, she was hired to be the international marketing manager for a high-end fashion house. It was her consistent action that finally brought her the start of a whole new career. Keeping her banking job during all this made it quite a challenge, but giving herself the permission to pursue what she really wanted kept her going.

Like Joyce's, your plan may include retraining or even sprucing up rusty skills. Be willing to be a student again. You're accomplished, you're successful, and sometimes feeling stupid is enough to make you quit. Don't! You're making an investment in yourself that will pay off in your own sense of fulfillment and happiness. You can't put a price on that. Getting your life reoriented around your internal wishes and expressing them is the greatest gift you can give to yourself and to the rest of us. When you express yourself, you're being yourself. There is nothing easier and more gratifying. Successful *and* happy—now that's a picture I can live with.

It's time to live YOUR life,
not the one that is expected of you.

Get What You Want and Want What You Have

▼

1. Recognize and give up external expectations.
2. Start living by your internal wishes (what you really want).
3. Identify your values.
4. Reorient your life and work around your values.
5. Create a crossover plan if you need to.
6. Schedule a weekly time to review and strategize the implementation of your plan.
7. Get a lot of support.
8. Celebrate your new life!

Caught in Survival Mode— How to Get Out and Become the Rainmaker

"I'm doing everything I can.
I guess it's just not working."

I F YOU ARE RESPONSIBLE FOR BUSINESS DEVELOPMENT WITHIN AN organization, you are an intrapreneur—you are an entrepreneur inside another entity. You might be a lawyer, accountant, salesperson, or recruiter. Sarah was such a client. She was in her early fifties and had been with her executive recruiting firm for a year and a half when she came to work with me. She was bringing in $100,000 in revenues for the company, which yielded her a salary she was far from happy with. She was a junior partner in the firm and wanted to be a full-fledged partner. She felt down on her luck. She hoped that we could boost her efforts and her salary, and bring back her confidence. Our eighteen-month coaching relationship was a perpetual rocket ride. Each time we thought that we had hit a plateau, she sky-rocketed to the next level.

Sarah had been an employee of a large corporation before she came to work for this recruiting firm, and she had been making two big adjustments before she came to work with me. One was recruiting, which was a new business for her, and the other was being an intrapreneur. Learning to be in charge of every aspect of your business is a challenge for anybody doing it for the first time. When I met Sarah, two things were clear to me: First, she was in survival mode. She was settling for crumbs because she thought of herself as a rookie. She needed to start thinking bigger and to realize she could have the whole pie. Second, she needed to come up with systems for doing things and developing a systematic approach to her new business.

We examined everything she had been doing up until this point, and we came up with goals and an action plan so she could reach those goals. We created phone scripts for the cold calling she had to do and practiced for business development meetings. Most critical for Sarah was knowing what actions to take and when to take them. Because her business was still new and small, she had too much time on her hands, which led to less activity instead of more. With solid goals and numbers to hit, she was able to create a structure that supported her to be her best. For example, she knew she had to make at least three business development calls a day as well as answering urgent calls and do all her other work.

One of the biggest challenges for the intrapreneur, or sole entrepreneur, for that matter, is looking for new prospects while keeping up with day-to-day business. Although Sarah's three calls a day didn't sound like very many, they started the ball

rolling. Her confidence started to grow as the interest in her services increased. Her next step was to identify her ideal client and start rejecting some smaller opportunities. She was afraid to do this at first, but the only way she would make her goal of raising her revenues to $300,000 was to start going for bigger searches. Her standards kept on getting higher and higher, and she did not compromise them. By the time we had been working together for eight months, she had reached $800,000 in revenues and was taking home $300,000 in salary. Now she was fired up, and she wanted more.

As we rolled over into the next fiscal year, she set an even bigger income goal and started to find that she could put in less effort to get the same results. She now had time for having fun, and she had a more balanced life. As she created more infrastructure to support the volume she had started to bring in, she had the freedom to take even bigger and smarter actions to make her business grow. She focused on relationships with current clients and arranged to go on retainer with one of them. She also worked with me to be more visible in her industry. She started to do public speaking and was written up in several magazines, which built her reputation even more. She is now often sought by the media to comment on the job market and the technology industry, which is her specialty.

Repeat business became the norm for Sarah. Her list of reliable accounts was growing. She never burned bridges, and she was generous with her time, with both clients and job candidates. This came back to her tenfold, as candidates who got placed in high-level positions turned around and hired her to perform searches for their organizations. She was now the rainmaker. She brought in the business, and her support system executed most of it. With each month that passed, she kept thinking bigger and bigger, until the results seemed to come without effort.

Eighteen months after starting, Sarah has increased her income even further and is just shy of her revenue goal of $1 million for this fiscal year. She is a successful intrapreneur with a rich life and the feeling of peace that comes from knowing that she just has to be herself to attract the results that she wants. She puts in as many hours as the next person, but it works and it's easy, just as it should be. It's all the result of the choices she made.

Are you wondering if you might be in the wrong business, or if you're just not good enough at what you do, because things aren't going as they should? You may be right, but before you try anything else, think about this: You are limited by the choices you've made and by how little you have valued yourself. That's a big assumption on my part, but I'll take the risk and say that before you write off your job, profession, or yourself, you should take a look at how small your thinking has been. Sometimes mediocre results come from aiming too low. You settled for surviving. You need to be playing a bigger game, and that game starts with you and with allowing yourself to think big. You may have limited yourself and cut off your potential at the knees by not expecting enough of yourself.

Marianne was a beautiful, charming woman who had aspirations to be an actress and a model. She had never made more than $30,000 a year. She took work as a catering waitress to get by, and she took any bit acting role or modeling gig she could get. No self-respecting actress/model in New York City could expect anything different from a tough, competitive business. Until she hired a coach, that is. She hated catering work, so I re-

quested that she stop doing it immediately. She thought I was crazy, because that was how she survived. Ah, true, but only because she was not expecting enough of herself. I wasn't convinced yet that she really believed that she could make it in acting or modeling.

Her next step was to refuse any acting work that was not up to par or didn't pay what she thought was a fair wage. She used to take whatever she could get because she needed the money or felt she needed the experience. Bah, humbug; she just didn't think she was capable of more. In modeling, I asked her to raise her standards and not to take any work that did not pay her what she wanted. She considered my requests carefully, and little by little she was able to make changes. It took seven months for her to make the transition from expecting very little to expecting the best. In the end, she landed an $85,000-a-year modeling contract. I'd say that is just the beginning, if she wants it to be. She only needs to keep thinking big and to keep being responsible by taking the actions that will reel in the results she wants.

So where are you selling yourself short? Where are you at the mercy of the picture you have created? Where are you stopped from believing there is more for you? Allow me to introduce you to the Fish Tank Theory. The Fish Tank Theory says that tropical fish can only grow as big as their tanks; if you put them in a bigger tank, they will grow to accommodate that tank. What does that have to do with you? The Fish Tank Theory works with humans too.

My husband introduced me to the theory twice before I started applying it to businesses and to my clients. Twice in our life as a couple, we have changed "fish tanks," with amazing growth as a result. The first time, when we married, we moved from a studio apartment to a one-bedroom apartment. We were doubling our expenses and very nervous about making such a big leap. We moved to our bigger tank, and within months both our incomes grew to accommodate it. It was even more dramatic when we moved from that one bedroom into our first home; we were taking a big leap, knowing we were not being foolish, but taking a big risk, just the same. Again, in a few short months we grew to accommodate the new tank, and we never felt a pinch. Now we drive by modest mansions, getting ideas about our next tank. This is a literal version of the theory—we actually changed the tank we lived in. More figuratively, the Fish Tank Theory works in business and in your career, as you create the next step to grow into.

Designing the next tank has an effect like that of having a vision. When you can see it, you can reel it in. When you can define it clearly, you can draw it to you. Designing a tank means creating a picture for your business or life that you can grow into. The clearer and more specific it is, the more likely you are to achieve it. It means stretching for something that is a next step even before you're really ready for it. It requires a leap of faith and yet it is not foolish.

The Fish Tank Theory can only work on calculated risk. If your next tank is outrageously huge, irrational, and a pipe dream, you are likely to jump into the new tank and drown. The next tank can be a risk, maybe even a little frightening, but it can't bury you. With that said, let's take the Fish Tank Theory and make it work for you. Let's design your tank.

THE 1-3-5 PLAN

The 1-3-5 plan will help you design your tank. 1-3-5 stands for one-year, three-year, and five-year plans. Start with the five-year plan. Where would you like to be in five years? If you're like many people, you may be stuck for an image or even a clue as to where you'd want to be so far from now. That's OK; we're writing fiction here. It's not here yet; neither is tomorrow. Any plan is fiction, but we can work from images to create reality. You have to see it before you can achieve it. Be wild; don't be afraid to think big. It's safe to think wildly about five years from now; we'll rein it in later. As Donald Trump once said, "If you're going to be thinking anyway, you might as well think big."

Success by Design: The Plan

Design your five-year plan. Describe what it looks like from every angle. How much money will you be making? Where will you be living? What kind of office will you be working in? Who will be working there with you? What will your family life look like? How will you do business (i.e., presentations, shows, cold calling, public relations, mailings, media, profit centers, products)?

When you have your five-year plan, do the same for the three-year and one-year plans. Remember to include the activities you will be doing in your business and details for every aspect of your life. What has to happen in year three to yield year five? What has to happen in year one to yield year three?

I would venture to guess that your one-year plan is now much bigger than it would have been if you had done the one-year plan first. Now you're creating a fish tank to grow into. Can you handle it? Where do you need to change, grow, or adjust to get on a track toward fulfilling your plan for year one?

Imagine yourself on the top of a mountain where your vision is unobstructed for miles around. From here, you can see your one-, three-, and five-year plans clearly. You are in the strategic position; you are the CEO of your plan. You have completed this part in just having sketched your 1-3-5. The next place to be is in the middle of the mountain—you are management, and you need to perform the tasks that will help you reach the strategic goals. This will determine what action you need to take in the first one to three months to reach your vision. Write down what these actions should be. The last place is at the bottom of the mountain, where you determine what tasks need to be performed on a daily, weekly, and monthly basis to fulfill what the management at the middle of the mountain needs.

As you start implementing your plans, keep this image in mind to help you figure out which action has to get done, when and in which order, to get you where you want to go. Sarah used this to get the structure in place to build her portion of the firm's business. As an intrapreneur, you need to know all these pieces, even if you have a good support system in place. Once you have your plan, you can put yourself back at the helm and get going.

IDEAL CLIENTS

Now that you have your own informal business plan, we will need to add a couple of layers to the mix to put you at the top of your game. If you are to become the rainmaker, you'll have to keep thinking bigger, raising your standards along the way. Sarah chose to work with only ideal clients; that was one of the things that pulled her ahead. Well, you're next. Who is your ideal client? You know the ones. They are easy to work with, they don't nickel-and-dime you, they trust your judgment, and send you referrals. Take the time to write down *your* ideal client profile. Make it clear and concise. What three or four things do you need to feel great about working with someone?

The biggest downfall of intrapreneurs and entrepreneurs is that they are willing to work with anyone who wants them. Whether you're selling a product or a service, taking on a client that does not fit your ideal client profile is usually more trouble than it's worth. These clients are usually the ones you do double the work for, and they are still not satisfied. If you take a close look at your client roster, you will also see that problem clients refer clients just like them—more problem clients. Lucky you. With the time and energy you would save by not working with them, you could attract two more clients that you *do* want to work with. You need to get problems out of your life for good. The solution is to work only with ideal clients.

"I'm supposed to deal with my customers' problems; that's what I'm paid for." No, you're paid to do a great job and bring in business, not to be a problem-solving wreck. I know I am asking a lot of you by directing you to work only with ideal clients. The usual response is "I'd have to let go of at least half of my clients." That's interesting; no wonder you feel like you're dragging a lead weight and can't rise to the top. A radical action would be to let them go. A less radical action would be to drop some and to teach those that are educable how to become ideal clients.

One of my clients works for a big brokerage house. He wants to change his fee structure from commission to fee-based. His ideal clients will be those that will go fee-based with him because that is how he wants to work. Suddenly, three-fourths of his clientele are no longer ideal clients. He is in the process of reeducating them. He knows he may lose some in the crossover, but it is a risk he is willing to take to get to where he wants to go.

Working with ideal clients will bump you up to the next level, but you are ready for more. Let's raise the stakes. Sarah chose her ideal client, but she also raised the stakes. She was no longer satisfied with $40,000 or $50,000 searches. She declared that she would only do $100,000 and above. As it turned out, it was above, period. To everything else, she said no. This is the next step for you. What's your bigger game? It could be a bigger-ticket item, a different product or service, or handling more volume. Just start stretching. A prospective client was responsible for business development and felt that he was working hard, but his numbers did not add up. I asked him if he knew where the bigger clients were. He said yes. I asked him why he was not talking to those people. There was a long silence at the other end of the phone. I can only guess that was all the coaching he needed because I never heard from him again, but I know in my gut he got what I was trying to say.

SYSTEMATIZING

Now I do have to warn you about a problem with the "play the bigger game" mentality. As you take on more volume or take on a bigger type of client that requires more work, you're going to need more help. Sarah needed more people to help her execute the searches, and this cost money. She had to lobby her firm to allow her more infrastructure. Without it, she still would have gotten the bigger clients, but they would not have given her repeat business if she couldn't deliver excellent service.

To avoid growing pains, it will be important for you to have specific systems that will be passed on as you delegate pieces of your business to other people. You will need to sit down and write out what you do and the order in which you do it until you have a system that someone else can follow. Your description has to be so detailed that if you disappeared tomorrow, someone could sit at your desk, read your system notes, and do your job. Most of us are good at what we do and have no idea that there is a system to it; we just do what we do. Nevertheless, to make your business grow beyond what you alone can accomplish in a day, you will need to duplicate yourself by having very strong systems. You need to be able to give pieces of work away painlessly. The purpose of a system is to free you to do only the parts of your work in which you are brilliant.

As you grow, it will also be important for you to track your business relationships. As you start doing more and more business, it will be harder to keep up your contacts. Here is room for another system: Never be more than one month away from your valuable contacts. Send them articles on your industry or, better yet, theirs. Send them a fax. Distribute a friendly, newsy memo from your office. Get in the press and send them your clippings. Whatever you do, stay current with them, no matter how busy you get. When you do so, they are reminded of you, and yours will be the number they call when they need your product or service. Don't sell yourself; just keep building the relationships.

ASKING FOR WHAT YOU'RE WORTH OR MORE

Asking for what you are worth—this is the moment of truth, a scary moment for some, because you always risk rejection. There is only one way to find out, and it is very, very good for you: Ask, ask, ask. You will find your limits more quickly than if you make assumptions about them. Of course, there is this prevalent question: "How do I know what I'm worth?" Your gut will tell you. When you have undersold yourself, you know it almost immediately by that sick feeling in your stomach. Another sign is the dread that comes over you before you meet with a client who is less than ideal. Don't confuse nervousness or intimidation with dread. That feeling in the pit of your stomach is a sign that you are doing something you don't really want to do. So, with that said, how do you ask for what you're worth or more?

If I haven't said it before, let me say it now. "No" is one of the most powerful words you can use when it comes to getting what you want. So is "yes," but most people will say yes to their own detriment before they say no. No, when used properly, then opens the way for yes. To explain: You want the work or the job order. It's not an ideal client, or it's really a small account, but what the heck, it's better than nothing. No. If you're too busy with "better-than-nothings," you could be too busy to seize the opportunity that may come later and really matter. I know the arguments to this one. "One in the hand is better than two in the bush." "They could grow to be bigger clients." "If they give me this, maybe we'll do something better the next time." All this is true, but I am assuming you can afford to take risks. If you're desperate, you'll have to do anything it takes to survive, but if you're not, you have room to push the envelope.

Sarah now wouldn't dream of taking the kind of searches she did in the beginning because now she doesn't have to. However, long before she became the rainmaker, she played this way with me. She said no, not knowing where the next good client would come from, but lo and behold, it did come, and she got to say yes, a lot. She never let up. How about you? Can you afford to do this? Do you believe in yourself enough to know you can make this happen? It's scary in the beginning, but when you start seeing that you can be successful on your own terms, you will be so glad you went through it.

Greg is a perfect example of how saying no grew his business and got him what he was worth. In the telecommunications company in which he worked, Greg had assigned accounts as well as those he drummed up on his own. His boss wanted to give him an account that was less than ideal. Of course, he was expected to say yes, but he said no instead. He ruffled a few feathers, but he explained that he knew he was capable of more and that this account would keep him from what he knew he could produce. His boss backed off, and within no time Greg brought in two sizable accounts that put him on the boards as a top producer. He had said no and made way for not only one but two big yeses.

Do you know what is acceptable and unacceptable to you? Do you find out after the fact that you should have said no to something? Do you know how to ask for what you're worth and stick to it? Define where you stand with this. What do you want? What are you willing to do to get it? If you ever feel dread about meeting a client or about doing some part of your job, you have hit on something unacceptable for you. Use this as a sign to help you determine when you will say no from now on so you are free to say yes to what will make you a rainmaker.

> The more you define *yourself*,
> the more business will soar.

Go from Being Jammed to Being a Rainmaker
▼

1. Think BIG.
2. Create your new fish tank.
3. Map it in a 1-3-5-year plan.
4. Choose your ideal client.
5. Play a bigger game (tighten up the infrastructure accordingly).
6. Ask for what you're worth or more.
7. Go out and play in the rain!

SIX

New at Entrepreneurship—
Going from Hobby to Critical Mass

"I don't know how I'll ever make the transition from a home-based start-up to a full-fledged business."

JAY WAS A WELL-EDUCATED AND EXPERIENCED BUSINESSMAN IN HIS forties who had left a position as a VP of sales and marketing in a major company to start his own consulting company. His company had been through a reorganization, and there was a chance he could lose his job, so when his wife got a great job offer that meant moving to another city, he decided it was a good time to make the change. He had been in business for a year when he hired me to help him grow it. He had only netted $15,000 in the first year, and he wanted to give it everything he could moving forward.

It was hard enough to start a business from scratch, but having also moved to a city where he knew very few people, Jay had had a very rough first year. Although his wife made enough money to support the family, things were taking longer than they had hoped, and tension was starting to grow between them. Our first job was to adjust their expectations and to make a reasonable plan about how long it would take him to build his business. Also, it was clear to me that his network needed to grow exponentially for him to do the kind of business he wanted to do. Until now, he had worked with small companies, advising them on their marketing plans and executing some of these plans for his clients. Where he wanted to be was inside corporations, working as a market research consultant. He needed to build a reputation doing what he wanted to do, although he had not done it before. He kept his small business clients as we worked on building his network and getting him where he wanted to go.

Within weeks he had looked into every professional group there was in the city, and he started to attend meetings of the ones that looked interesting to him. Over the course of his first year with me, he increased his database from fifty to four hundred names. He had started a marketing newsletter, which he distributed at no cost, to start getting his name out there. One of the people who read his newsletter was someone in the first company that set him in the direction he wanted to go. He worked as a market research consultant to a new technology start-up that involved him in constructing its marketing strategy. As he continued to network, he was able to leverage this job to get an exclusive contract with a large ad agency that outsourced its research to him. By the end of his second year in business, he was still working out of his house, but he had an assistant and was able to draw a $60,000 salary.

By the time Jay's business was two and a half years old, he started to hit critical mass. He knew a number of influential people, so work started to come to him more quickly than he could keep up with it. He decided it was time to take his business outside his home, so he found an office space and hired another person. He now had an administrative person and someone who could help him with research. His marketing newsletter became so popular that he could not keep up with the demand for free, so he turned it into another profit center for himself. He wrote it, someone else produced it, and it was a form of passive income. His original clients became honorary recipients of the newsletter at no charge, for as long as they wanted it. Jay wanted to show his appreciation for his roots, so to speak. He also decided to not let his old market go altogether. Although he no longer consulted with small businesses on their marketing, they still sought him out. He saw this as another opportunity to have passive income, so he created an audiocassette series for that segment of his market. They couldn't get Jay himself, but they could have his system for creating a marketing plan for their businesses.

By the time he finished his third year in business and we wrapped up our relationship, he had over eight thousand contacts, which he had generated through his newsletter's exposure. He had drawn a $120,000 salary, and he had projected sales for the next year at $1 million. His business was not a hobby anymore.

Welcome to the wacky world of entrepreneurship. Do you have what it takes? You have to believe that you do, if you want to make it work. Entrepreneurship is the new American dream—telling the boss to stuff it and going out on your own. Some of you may have been forced out on your own through downsizing or long bouts with the unemployment office. However you got here, you'll want to make sure you have what it takes to stay here. Are you ready? What I want for you is a thriving, successful business. Let's get you out of the hobby stage and into making more money. There is nothing more demeaning than someone saying, "Oh, you're a consultant. How long have you been unemployed?" Let's show them who they are dealing with.

Attitude and perseverance are half the battle. The other half is having a winning strategy and plan for your business. Layered on both of these is your ability to make an impact on people and get them to talk about you. Where do you stand in these three areas? Which needs the most improvement? Where do you sabotage yourself the most? Don't make that face. We all sabotage ourselves somewhere along the line. Admitting it and coming up with a great way to fix it is the healthiest way to go. Denying it gets you nowhere.

ARE YOU AN ENTREPRENEUR?

Just having your own business doesn't guarantee that you are an entrepreneur. Successful business owners have certain characteristics that help make them successful. Being an entrepreneur doesn't mean that you have to reach the scope of a Bill Gates or Martha Stewart, but you do need a set of characteristics that can make it possible for you to generate and sustain a successful venture. Consider these questions to find the entrepreneur in you:

Can you pull yourself out of bed in the morning knowing only you will give your day structure?

Can you deal with extreme isolation and absolutely no external accountability?

Can you handle it if your great idea flops in the
marketplace?

Do you have enough chutzpah and cash to take calculated
risks?

Do you know when to bail out?

Are you willing and able to ask for help?

Are you impossible to intimidate?

Would you rather die than fail?

Are you willing to fail to learn?

Are you flexible enough to do a 180 at the drop of a dime?

Do you think far enough ahead to avoid pitfalls?

Are you able to see five years from now?

Do you think you can avoid losing your life to a business?

Are you a cockeyed optimist who sees the downside of
everything?

This is by no means a definitive list, but if you answered yes
to each of these questions, you've got the paradoxical qualities
and seemingly mutually exclusive traits of the successful entrepreneur. If you answered no to any of them, you've got some
work to do. You may need a partner who has some of the at-
tributes that you don't, or you will need to find a way to improve
in these areas. Look for role models, read about successful entrepreneurs, participate in self-improvement work, and hire a
coach.

MONEY

Foremost on everyone's mind and crucial for the self-employed:
money. Who is financing this business? If you are hocking your

savings to start this venture, how long can you go before you will be in trouble? If you plan to borrow, do you have a solid plan that will impress banks and investors? You will need a solid business plan regardless of who will finance your business. Just as you have been directed in previous chapters to write out your goals, the business plan serves the same purpose. It's a map to guide you to where you want to go. Many people start a business without one; it's not a federal offense, but it will catch up with you eventually, once you have hit a certain level of success. Get in the habit of business planning now, and avoid the train wreck later on. There are great resources in libraries and bookstores to help you do this. If the level of detail in this work is going to stop you from doing it, delegate it.

I was speaking recently at a gathering of an organization devoted to women business owners, and a woman stood up at the end when I asked people to share what they could now do, based on what they had heard. She exclaimed jubilantly that she could now give herself permission to delegate her business plan. She had been struggling with it for months and felt like she was going to fail at the whole venture because she couldn't write the plan. She got my message, and I hope you do too. Being in business for yourself doesn't mean strife and struggle; it means knowing what you do well and getting help with the rest.

Where I started with all this was money; you're going to need a reserve of it. My experience is in service businesses, and it takes a solid one to three years to get to a place where such a business builds critical mass and takes off. You are going to need at least six to twelve months' expenses for your business and for yourself to avoid having desperation color your business. Don't even think about starting without having this financial reserve. I don't care how sure you are that you are going to succeed; banking on a miracle is too big a risk to take. Don't do that to yourself, to your family, and to your long-term financial and mental health. If need be, get a mindless part-time job to keep your financial integrity. And for you, the one rolling your eyes knowing you don't have to listen to this because you're going to go ahead anyway, I challenge you to have your business be profitable from day one. Go ahead. Do it with no cushion, but don't go in the red. Actually, this is a point for every business owner, no matter what your risk tolerance is. Design your business to be profit driven rather than revenue driven. Bringing in $500,000 is not that impressive if you spend $495,000 of it. Plan your business conservatively so that you can rely on profits to make improvements and promote growth instead of incurring debt to do so.

Leslie started her consulting business on a shoestring budget. When she started out, she invested in such necessary items as telephone, fax, business cards, and inexpensive but presentable promotional materials. As she made more money, she spent more on her business. The additional phone lines, better-quality stationery, a nicer brochure, an assistant, and additional products came from her profits as she could afford them. She never borrowed a cent and still managed to double her income every year for the three we worked together. Many entrepreneurs are deluded into thinking that they have to spend a lot of money to get started and have the best of everything. I appreciate your wanting to have the best, but be mindful of when it's wasteful. For example, take a brochure: You start your new business, you spend a fortune creating an image, you put together a classy brochure, and within six months it no longer represents you and you need a new one. If you had waited, you would have saved a lot of money. Unless you have done extensive market research (which I recommend you do, but most small business owners overlook this), it takes a while to get the kinks out of a new business and really know that what you are putting into the marketplace is going to work. Save the big bucks until you really know what you want to do. In the meanwhile, make it on what you have, always keep a reserve of money, and get it into your head that getting by is not good enough; you should be making more than enough to get by.

WHAT DO YOU DO?

What do you do? Can you answer it in one sentence? If you can't, you are not alone. I have worked with several hundred people, and many have the same problem. Yet it has proved to be the most effective way to increase their businesses—to identify what they really do and to communicate it clearly. Don't make the mistake of using a label or a long-winded explanation to educate people about what you do. How many times has that inspired someone to say "That's exactly what I need!"? Imagine a sentence so powerful that people "buy" on the spot, or they talk about you to the next person they meet who could use you or your service. That sentence is your point of recognition. It tells people what the result will be if they work with you. That sentence is the point at which your customers recognize that you are the answer to their prayers. You want them to respond with "I need that," or "How do you do that?" or "Who couldn't use that?!"

Your Point of Recognition

Write out the results that people achieve by purchasing your product or service. Don't focus on the product or service itself or how you achieve the results for your clients; just tell them how they will benefit. Think of it in terms of their needs. What do they need that you provide the solution to? Write down twenty results, and then add above the list: "I work with people who _____" or "I work with companies that want _____." When you narrow it down to a few, start trying them out on people and see how they respond. When you start hearing oohs and ahs, you know you have found your point of recognition.

Your point of recognition will become your calling card. It has to be simple so that people can repeat it easily. I knew mine was working the day a referral called and said, "I spoke to Diana, who said that you help people take their personal and professional life to the next level." The next phone call was from the person who had made the referral. She said, "Lynn is going to call you. I told her you help people take their personal and professional life to the next level." Bingo! It's repeatable, and it's out there working for me without my being present. Daniel, a TV commercial producer, says, "We work with agencies that want a $250K commercial for $100K." Rita, a managed-care consultant, says, "I work with doctors who want a guide through the managed-care maze." Richard, an independent insurance broker, says, "I work with people who want to protect their family and their assets." Do you get the idea?

Watch out for promises that make people skeptical. You can say that you work with people who want to make more money or with companies that want to have an impact on their bottom line, but that's true of everyone. It goes in one ear and out the other. You'll have to find another way. You'll also want to be careful not to confuse your point of recognition with a slogan. Slogans sound kind of cute, and your point of recognition is much more powerful. You wouldn't want something like "We work with people who want to go where the everyman won't go." You don't need anything cute, just a solid statement of the outcome that becomes the point at which customers recognize that they need you.

NETWORKING

For every business owner, it is not so much who you know, but rather, who knows you. Until you can afford recognition for your product or service through major advertising dollars, you will be its best commercial. Get off your butt and meet, meet, meet. To do this effectively, you will need to learn to become a master networker. Now, I didn't say master schmoozer or master shark, two images that often come up for people when they have to think of going out in the world for the purpose of meeting people to do business with. Networking is like matchmaking; you connect people you know with people they don't know, and they do the same for you. The connections always have a specific purpose: to help each other in business or in achieving goals. It only feels schmoozy or scheming if there is no genuine connection between you, and that is what you will want to avoid from the start.

You network to build relationships, not necessarily to count how many cards you've collected by the end of a luncheon. You'll have to stop yourself from having "What can they do for me?" at the forefront of your mind. Turn it around. Put the people ahead of what you want from them. Become a resource to the people you meet. You are the expert in your industry or service; use that to serve other people. They might become your clients, but if they don't, you might help them get something they need. That will put you at the forefront of their minds when they meet someone who could be your client. The point is to listen to what they need as intently as you would ask for what you need, and you will have to ask. As much as you might wish they were, people are not mind readers. If you don't ask for what you need, they will assume you need nothing. Sad, but true. Being specific about your requests will be most important. "I'm looking for good prospects for my business" isn't as specific as "My ideal client is someone who is looking to take his business to the next level."

I learned one of my favorite things to keep in mind about networking from a book called *Power Networking* (Mountain-Harbour Publications, 1992), by my colleague Sandy Vilas, co-written with Donna Fisher. They describe the Three Foot Rule of networking, which says that anyone within three feet of you is someone you can network with. Unless you live in a very rural area, you have the potential to be networking with a lot of people. When I first started my business, the subways of New York City were a very successful networking location for me. Many long-term supporters and participants in my workshops are people I met by chatting on the subway. Even a couple of movie and TV celebrities sent me referrals, based on our subway conversations. These were just casual conversations, not sell jobs. "What do you do?" always comes up, and the right point of recognition is the clincher. "Oh, I could use that" or "I know someone who needs that; give me your card." If you are open to it, you never know what can happen.

Your first instinct will probably be to meet as many people as possible—not a bad instinct at all, but soon you'll discover it is not so easy to keep up with that many people. Not to worry; you're ready for the next level of networking. You will probably work with as many clients as you can get your hands on and eventually get choosier until you work only with ideal clients; so goes the networking game. The ideal client in networking is your center of influence. These people know you and what you do, and they happen to come in contact with many others who could use your service or product. These are the people you want to invest in. These are the people who should hear from you often in one way or another. These are the people you can gladly spend your time and resources on. For example, a strong relationship with an accountant when you are a financial advisor could be beneficial for both of you. If you invest most of your energy in ten centers of influence, keeping in mind that there are a hundred or more people behind each of them, you have the start of a very healthy referral-generating network. What are you waiting for? I don't care if you have to start with one center of influence. Get out there and find them.

You've now started building relationships, developing centers of influence, and meeting the people they have connected you to. If they haven't become your customers yet, what do you do with them? You have to give them another chance to become your customers. How do you do that? Find ways for people to sample your product or service or to get a better idea of what you are about. Jay, in the example, started his newsletter for this very purpose. He didn't sell himself in it; he just offered valuable information to his would-be clients that positioned him as a resource to them. He was the one they called when the newsletter sparked an interest or a need. This was how he let people get a taste of who he was and what he could offer. The newsletter served his would-be customers. It helped build a reputation and, eventually, a clientele. It also became a profit center and a source of passive income. You will want to be looking for additional profit centers and ways to have passive income as well.

In terms of samples, how might you give your customers a trial run? Does your business lend itself to a free consultation? To writing articles? To delivering free or low-cost workshops on the topics that might interest your prospects? Do you have a Web site? (If you don't, why not?) Make sure it educates your prospects by doing more than just telling them about your product or service. Tell them about themselves. For example, if you are a marketing consultant, don't tell them what you do; instead ask your prospects about their marketing. "Do you have a marketing plan? Do you get three calls a day from people who have heard about you? Does your business have one distinguishing feature that the public is aware of?" Get them thinking about themselves in a way that makes it impossible for them NOT to call you.

Tanya had her own firm; she wrote corporate communications and speeches for executives. She was especially interested in increasing the number of speeches she wrote per year, and she wasn't sure how to let people know that. We saw this as a great opportunity to do an educational Web site. Working with a Web designer, Tanya created original ways to give people pointers about their speeches and speaking style through inter-active instruction on her site. She directed people to her Web site through mailings and postings on the Internet. It took a while for people to catch on, but soon she had writing assign-ments for much higher-level clients. Invitations to speak also started to roll in. She overcame her own fear of public speaking by creating a workshop based on her tips for writing and giving speeches. This has been another way for people to sample her and to learn about what she can do for them.

ADDING VALUE

Whether it be perceived or actual, it will become essential for you to add value to your product or service to keep you mov-ing toward building critical mass. We want to get you to the point at which business just comes in, seemingly on its own—where it feels like you don't have to work so hard to get busi-ness, but rather are spending your time delivering the product or service that inspired you to go into business in the first place. To add value to that, you must serve your clients even better than they expected you to. It doesn't mean showering them with more things that cost you money, but rather finding ways that may not cost anything to make you more valuable to them.

When was the last time you talked to your customers about their needs? Was it when they first were considering hiring you? It's time to talk to them again. You can easily add value to what you offer by having your customers give you input on what else they need. If they help you design it, how could you not be adding value directly to them? They will also feel more included, which will raise your popularity. That could mean more referrals.

You can add value by making it a privilege to be part of the "family" that buys or uses you. Saturn cars is the best big-business example of this. Saturn goes out of its way to create a community around buying this car. If you are a Saturn owner, you could be featured in one of their ads or commercials. Even after the fact, they offer special classes and gatherings to educate you about their product. They make it a privilege to be their customer. They don't do these things for the people that aren't their customers yet. Bring this idea into your small business. What special privileges can you make available to clients only, to add value to being your client? It may be something as simple as your own Rolodex. If you're able to take care of many of their needs, even those you can't meet by giving referrals, this is a great plus. You might also run free seminars for clients and their guests, pass on valuable business information through e-mail, or write articles on topics of interest as another way to add value.

When clients work with you or buy something from you, where does your vision for them end? When they buy? When they send you business or become repeat customers? Take customers beyond what you can do for them and into what they can do for themselves, to add even more value. I mean that you can challenge them to make more money or to become more because they now have your product or service. For example, if people hire me as their coach, I ask them: "What will you do differently now that you have a coach?" "What are you willing to go for that you would not have gone for before?" If clients buy your product, challenge them and help them to come up with ways to make more money because they have it. This also applies if you offer a service. This makes what you offer that much more valuable.

Another way to add value has less to do with adding something and more to do with taking something away. If you make your product or service more exclusive, you can actually add value to it. If you raise your fees or your standards or develop a strong niche, you will exclude some people from your business, but those who are included in that group will value your business even more. Some customers won't buy if the prices are too low or if there is nothing special about what you do. If you're exclusive, that makes them part of a select group, and many people will pay more for that. If you're too cheap, they might think there's a catch or that something must be wrong if your product or service is not worth more. The only person stopping you from this is you. Where do you need to invest in yourself to feel ready to get more exclusive with what you offer? Where could you learn something new, add a feature, or appear more valuable to your customer? If a watch is just a watch, why do people go out of their way to buy something marked Cartier or Rolex?

GETTING MORE OUT OF YOUR BUSINESS

The most difficult thing for entrepreneurs, after finding seed money, is to enjoy the quality of life they wanted when they went into their own business. You might have left your job thinking, "If I'm going to work this hard, I might as well do it for myself and have the time to be able to finally enjoy the fruits of my labor." There is no doubt that there is a great level of satisfaction in running your own show, but if it becomes a twenty-four-hour-a-day, seven-day-a-week proposition, you're really not enjoying anything. Of course, being in business for yourself requires hustle, determination, and sometimes extra hours. However, when it becomes a way of life, or even yet, *becomes* your life, it can't really be worth it. What I want for you is what you've been reading about throughout this book: a successful business and a great life. The more balance you are able to strike between the two, the easier your success will be.

If you let your business spread into an around-the-clock event, it will be hard to come back from that. The only way to go is to set it up right from the start. If you work out an ideal work schedule instead of letting work take up progressively more room, you will force yourself to come up with the bigger and better action to do it in less time. Managing your time will become critical. If you're ready to get more out of your business by giving it less of your time, pay attention to the following:

1) **Mark your territory.** Have a place to do business that is your own. If you don't run an office outside your home, make sure your area in the home is used exclusively for work. This minimizes distractions and helps you physically mark where home ends and business begins.

2) **Create your ideal work schedule.** Block off the times you would like to devote to work and the times you want to devote to other things, and never let the two overlap. Make that schedule work. If you must do more, look at it as overtime, don't allow it to become routine.

3) **Schedule for emergencies.** Leave room in your schedule for the unexpected. (The unexpected is quite reliable.) If you don't

leave gaps in your schedule, you will end up working all the time.

4) Create iron-solid boundaries. You will have to protect your working time like a mother bear protects her cubs. When you work for yourself (especially if you're home-based), friends and relatives think it's OK to call to chat. You will have to make it very clear that you are working and let them know when your time is off-limits to them. Let them know when you will be off the clock. This goes for kids or for anyone else who might be vying for your attention.

5) Create a daily framework. Make a list of all the things that you wish you could do during the course of the day but that usually get pushed aside because of a lack of time. They are usually the very things that would make all the difference to your professional and personal well-being. They should become the framework of your day. They should be the constants that the rest of the day revolves around—for example, making five business development calls a day, cleaning your desk at the end of the day, spending quality time with the kids, catching up with your spouse, exercising, logging follow-up calls, and so on. Make a list of important items; plan the rest of the day around them.

6) Create a single daily action. Your single daily action is the one thing that, if you did nothing else all day, could keep your business moving forward. For most, it's some kind of business development goal. Most people hate having to make those calls. If that's you, do it first; get it out of the way. Your single daily action is the constant that must happen even if the rest of the day gets snafu'd. A general rule of thumb for time management is: If you dread it, do it first.

7) **Build on your strengths and delegate your weaknesses.** Nothing will move your business along faster and keep you saner than delegating every part of your business at which you are not a genius. Even if you think you cannot afford the help, get creative and find it. All those people who want a piece of you in your life would probably love to be included by doing pieces of your business that you don't want to do or don't have the time to do. Anyone can do a mailing for you or return some phone calls or run an errand for you. In the early stages, when a new business can put a family in shock, make it less shocking by giving everyone an opportunity to help and to see what goes on in your business.

To get your business out of the hobby stage and into critical mass, you will need to be smart about your time and resources, and you will need to make the most of both of them without killing yourself in the process. I insist that it can be done, and that it does not have to be hard. You will have to be committed to the process and not hinge your well-being on results. Results will come, but you won't be able to control them as much as you think you can. Think of competitive swimmers in an Olympic-sized swimming pool. If they keep picking up their heads to see how far they have to go, they will fall behind. If they keep their heads in the water and make consistent strokes, they will make it to the wall. Be a swimmer; take consistent action in the areas we discussed, and you will do fine. You can get past being a hobby entrepreneur if you treat your business like a business from day one and are relentless in making the dream come true.

If you want a hobby, take up fishing. It's less taxing.

Entrepreneurship is the new American Dream.

Go from Hobby to Critical Mass

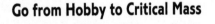

1. Make sure you are really an entrepreneur. If you're not, shore up the weak areas or find a partner who is strong in those areas.
2. Make sure you have enough money for six to twelve months of expenses.
3. Be profit driven rather than revenue driven.
4. Be able to answer "What do you do?" in one sentence. Develop your point of recognition.
5. Network your way to a great reputation. Develop centers of influence.
6. Add value to your product or service (and to yourself).
7. Get the most out of your business, so it doesn't get you. This is good time management.
8. Enjoy the American Dream.

SEVEN

On the Sales Roller Coaster— Smoothing Out the Ride

"When sales are good, life is good.
When sales stink, life stinks."

EVERYONE IS SELLING SOMETHING, BUT THOSE WHO MAKE A LIV-ing at it face a special set of circumstances that definitely keeps things interesting if nothing else. They deal with the addictive gush of adrenaline involved in "the chase," the even higher high of closing the deal, and the ever-present fear that each sale is the last. Most of you would probably wish for it to be a little less interesting sometimes. Smoothing out the roller-coaster ride would be nice, wouldn't it? This story will show you how to start:

Dennis was a sales professional whom I coached during the course of a year. He was thirty-six years old at the time and had a wife and two young children. He was a successful guy, but he was not incredibly happy doing what he was doing, and he decided to work with me to improve his performance all-around.

89

He seemed dissatisfied and frustrated, and he complained about a constant swing in his moods. When he did well at work, he was himself and a great dad and husband. When things didn't go his way at work, it colored his whole world. If his ups and downs had been more severe, I might have recommended that he work with a therapist, but this was something I have seen in many people whose income depends on sales, so we proceeded with that in mind.

Dennis's well-being was dependent on his performance at work because he was looking to get his personal needs met there. He was driven by a very powerful need that was satisfied when it was fed but made him miserable when it wasn't. In assessing his needs, we found that his most critical one was for recognition. This was his scenario; he looked at each prospect as a chance to get this need met. When he closed a sale, his need was met, and he would be on a high; but when he was faced with rejection, the personal toll was steep. He was coached to learn how to get this need met outside of sales relationships— by friends, trusted colleagues, and loved ones. It was awkward for him to admit to this need and to ask people he really trusted to recognize him for things that he did, regardless of how insignificant they seemed. As he started to experience the benefits of getting this need met in a positive way, he felt less vulnerable about admitting he had a need. "Everyone has needs, but not everyone is smart enough to get them met in a way that feels great," he realized. The inside effect was just one part of the reward; the other was what started to happen in his outside world.

When that need was met, Dennis developed an ease in his style, which produced a dramatic increase in closed sales. He upped his revenues by 40 percent and found even more recognition; he won several incentive prizes and was acknowledged at top-producer events. By not relying on his clients to meet his need for recognition, he was more able to be himself, and more likely to gain the business. His level of satisfaction went up too. Obviously, he was happy making more money and getting the recognition he wanted, but getting off the emotional roller coaster of making a living in sales helped him enjoy the work he was doing even more.

You wouldn't dare admit that you had a need for recognition, would you? You'd rather get it met any way you could rather than come right out and say you need the recognition, right? What a waste of time and energy. You'd have to resort to scheming and manipulating and proving something to pull that off. No thanks—I'd rather you understand that your needs are going to drive you no matter what. Getting them met is not optional. Thomas Leonard, a pioneer in the field of personal coaching, introduced me to this concept: Needs will run you, and they'll get met any way they can. "What is so bad about that?" you may ask. Well, you won't die from it; life will go on. But what if I told you it could be easier, that if your needs were met outside the sales and work environment, you might actually make more money? I bet I'd have your undivided attention. Have I got it now? Good. If you know what your critical needs are, you will have an insight into your motivation, which will help you perform better on the job. Once you get good at this for yourself, you will be much more insightful about what motivates your customers and colleagues. Your relationships will improve, and with them your business.

A life in sales is all about results. Too often your self-worth is attached to those results; your needs are met at work. If the results determine your well-being as a person, the results are too important, and this can make them more elusive. I know you've experienced this in your life: You're searching for the perfect mate. When you give up, exasperated, you find one. You're choking on the ball field. You figure you're a goner and stop trying. Bingo! You bounce back. The same is true of success in business. Make it easy, and you will do better. Getting your needs met can help you do that.

What are needs, anyway? They are what you *must* have to be your best. You're probably thinking, "What's so hard about that?" It doesn't sound complicated, but the things you need to be your best are probably exactly the things you would be embarrassed to come right out and ask for. Would you, like Dennis, ask for recognition? We've been pretty well trained to think that it's not appropriate to blatantly ask for what we need on that level. We're supposed to pretend we don't have any needs. None of us wants to feel needy, much less admit that we are, so you've probably never learned how to express your needs. Yet, as I said, needs will be met anyway. The trouble is that in their frenzy to get fed, needs can run amok and wreak havoc on your life, just as Dennis let them run amok all over his sales relationships. Your needs, whether you realize it or not, become the prism through which you see the world. They will skew how you see things, how you operate, and how you chase your own satisfaction. They will be met, consciously or unconsciously, so you might as well get conscious about them so you can fulfill your needs in ways that fuel you rather than rob you of your ability to achieve.

Randy was a successful man whose income depended on the sales he made. He had what looked like the perfect life: great wife, great kids, a beautiful home. He made a healthy six-figure income and had enough time to be at home every day for lunch and dinner as well as to play tennis or golf a few times during the workweek. He was also an avid gym goer and was in good health. Still, he was frustrated and restless; something was eating at him. My inkling was that he had an unmet need. We did the exercise you are about to do, and we discovered a huge need that was not being met—the need for autonomy.

As soon as he discovered this, even before he did anything about it, Randy was overcome with a huge sense of relief. "That's it! Now I get why I've been acting so weird for the last year or so," he said. Although he had a lot of downtime, he felt that every action needed to be reported either to his employees or to his family, and he had lost the sense of autonomy that was obviously critical to his being his best. He then proceeded to make the necessary changes to accommodate this need in a positive way. Until now, this need had been met unconsciously and negatively; he would snap at the people in his life or withdraw from those who needed his attention most.

Now it's your turn. What are your needs? Let's find out. No matter how successful you are, you can always become more successful if you have more information about yourself and about what makes you tick. Needs hold clues to who you are and what your vulnerabilities are. Once you know what they are, you can protect them. Write down your answers to the following questions. Keep in mind while you are doing so that you have many needs, but we want to identify your critical needs. You'll know which ones are critical, because they are the ones that rock your being. They have a Jekyll and Hyde–type effect on you. The needs that are the most crucial to your being your best cause you to feel great when they are met, and you feel out of sorts and act oddly when they are not met. To avoid being at the mercy of the downside, and to get to what's great about you, your work, and your life, your needs must be met. Get it?

NEEDS: HIDDEN HOT SPOTS

Take your time and write down your answers to the following questions:

1) **What drives you?** Is it money? Power? Attention? Position? Fame? Responsibility? Take a look at what need lies below the surface of what you just listed. If money drives you, is the underlying need the need for abundance? Prosperity? If you feel driven by power, what is the underlying need there? The need to control? The need to be the best? The need to be respected? Keep looking until you find the needs, and write them down.

2) **Where are you lacking in your life?** Where are you dissatisfied? What need is not being met? Once you are clear on what those needs are, write them down.

3) **What frustrates you?** What needs to be met to turn that around? Write down the needs.

4) **What do others think?** Ask three people whom you trust what they see as your critical needs. Ask a mentor, spouse, or close friend. Sometimes they can recognize your needs better than you can.

Here is a sampling of needs that might help with this exercise:

TO BE	TO HAVE
Accepted	Certainty
Included	Recognition
Appreciated	Accuracy
Valued	Autonomy
Cherished	Stability
Celebrated	Luxury
Listened to	Abundance
Accomplished	Power
Important	Peace
Independent	Honesty
Busy	Impact
Understood	Influence
Encouraged	Freedom
Preferred	Flexibility
Industrious	Pleasure
The Best	Dominance
Seen	Control
Loved	Results

Once you have gathered all this information, narrow your list of needs down to the three that are the most critical for you. Look at how you get these needs met now. Do you get them met in ways that fuel you or in ways that make things difficult for you?

Get ready to feed those tricky needs before they get you. How do you do that? As I said earlier, you might be tempted to have them met on the job. Since you spend most of your waking hours there, you would think that makes sense. Wrong; most workplaces are holding tanks for people trying to get their needs met. Conflict looms around every bend if you make that mistake. Clashing needs account for most interpersonal strain and worse. Do you work with any difficult or domineering people? What do you think they are trying to do? Yes, you guessed it; they are trying to get their needs met. Are they doing it right? No; but you will.

The first thing you'll need is a set of clear boundaries. You will need boundaries to keep other people from doing things that keep you from what you need. For instance, if you have a need for a certain level of respect and someone isn't giving you that, you will need to communicate how they need to change. (See chapter 2.) Even more important, however, will be setting up support systems where you can get your needs met effortlessly. I recommend that you save the workplace as the last place to do so, but it is by no means taboo.

DESIGNING SYSTEMS

It might be helpful to take a look at how some successful people became more successful by recognizing and taking action on their critical needs. A client who was a middle manager was feeling out of the loop at the office when a new team came in after a merger. He had a driving need to be the best, and before the new leadership came in, that need was met at work. In this new situation, that was no longer the case. Unfortunately, he started getting that need met in ways that were causing more harm than good. He would get in power struggles with people, and he felt competitive when he spoke to the new bosses. He did not feel comfortable, nor was it appropriate at the time, for him to discuss his needs openly, so we came up with a strategy that would help him be the best in as many places as he could, outside the work environment. He became fiercely competitive in his athletic pursuits. He told his trusted friends that he would be looking to excel at things that they did together, and he even brought being the best into his marriage—he wanted to be the best husband he could be. When he managed his needs this way, he became less competitive at work, which eventually helped him to become a more cohesive part of the team. Once the edge was off, he started to be noticed for his contributions, and he soon regained his feeling that he was the best at work too.

Pat was a committed business owner. She had been an advertising executive for many years and had gone out on her own two years before she came to work with me. Through doing the exercise you just did, we came to find that one of her critical needs was stability. She worked very hard to try to create stability as a sole proprietor in an unstable industry. She did not want to go back to a more stable corporate environment, so we created systems that would give her more stability in her life, thus taking the edge off her need to have her business supply it for her. She worked to save more money to feel more stable, and she told many people in her life about this need, so they would know that it was important that they be reliable and stable participants in her life. Her business grew by 30 percent during the year we worked together. This was a result both of her needs being taken care of and of several business-building actions we designed.

In another case, a sales manager found that his frustration with his own level of productivity and that of his team was driven by his need for industriousness. He needed to feel as if he were always producing, and as if his team were equally committed. As we set out to design a system by which this need could be satisfied, we found that he really had no idea what his team was doing. He was impatient with them and with himself because he had no connection to what they were doing, so he assumed they were not being productive. What worked to satisfy his need and to help him better communicate with his team was for them to e-mail him weekly reports at the end of each week. He saw that they were much more industrious than he had thought, and they didn't mind doing the reports once they saw his moods become more even. I also asked him to take a few minutes at the end of each day to write down what he had accomplished so he could see it. Without written documentation of his actions or those of his team, his need for industriousness led him into a daily frenzy. When he could see that things were getting accomplished, he calmed down and became much more effective.

Get creative, and enlist plenty of help in designing systems to help you meet your needs. It doesn't necessarily require radical change, but it does require thinking in terms of needs every time you hit a stumbling block. Ask yourself, "What need is not being met?" and get to work.

WHY BOTHER?

If getting your needs met seems like a lot of work, you're right, it is. However, once you do the work, you won't need to go through this again as long as you stay aware of what your needs are and keep them fed. When you are not driven by your needs, you can do a much easier, better job. We want sales to come to you instead of your feeling like you have to work so hard to get them. If your needs are met, it won't feel like such an uphill climb. Once that is handled, you can focus on your customers' needs, which will make buying from you much more attractive. You'll be more focused on them and less worried about landing them as clients. Let's get those customers rolling through your door. Getting your needs met was your first step in doing that, but you will need to do more to smooth out the sales roller coaster.

LISTENING

With your needs taken care of, you'll be less focused on yourself and better able to listen to your current or potential client. You've probably been trained to listen for what customers need so you can be the answer to their needs. That's good, but it's only the beginning. There is more to listening in a customer relationship than that. Do you really know how to listen? Yes, of course you do, or so you think. Do you *really* listen, so you can hear even what is not being said? That's the kind of listening I'm talking about. What I want for you are lasting client relationships, the kind that come from being a great people person and not just a slick salesperson. Think about it: Yes, people buy because you have something they need, but chances are they can get it from somebody else. So why do they buy? They buy because of who you are and what you bring to the equation. They will be even more likely to buy from you when they see something in you that they want for themselves. Maybe it's the way you communicate, the way you make them feel, the way you present yourself, the competency you display in your knowledge of the product and of them. It's something intangible about the way you are with them, and that something will start with how you listen and what you listen for.

What are you listening for when you speak to a prospect or customer? You're probably listening for the need or the sale, but I want you to listen *for* the person. Listen for *who* the person is. Remember what I said: You want to listen even for what they don't say, and that comes from focusing your attention on them and on anything you can learn about them as people. When you are trying to sell something, you are listening through a filter that says, "I can fix it. What I have is the answer."

When you are listening *for* people, your attention is on putting them ahead of the result. Be with them and with what they are up to. Acknowledge them and validate them.

I was speaking to the head of human resources for the eastern division of a national retail chain. We were discussing an executive who he thought could benefit from coaching. Before long, we were engaged in a light and casual conversation about his own job. When I put myself in his shoes and acknowledged what a challenging job he had, he opened up to me even more. By the time our conversation ended, he was ready to include himself in the coaching package he wanted to purchase and to talk about how we could work together on a more extended basis. That didn't happen because I was ready to pounce and make a sale. It happened because I listened to and for the person in such a way that he could see how I could be an asset to him. Granted, listening lends itself well to demonstrating coaching, but so does every industry that involves sales.

Here are four steps to becoming a better listener:

1) Become aware of the smokescreen you listen through. What runs through your mind when you are listening to someone?

Do you drift off? Do you get strong opinions running through your mind that go unsaid, like I agree/disagree, this is good/bad? Do you listen through a screen that says, "I am closing this account if it kills me"? These filters may be keeping you from the results you want. Become aware of them, and learn to get rid of them so you can pay attention.

2) Operate your mouth with a seven-second delay. Just as radio broadcasters keep words from hitting the airwaves for seven seconds to be sure they are listener-worthy, you can improve your listening by thinking twice if you really need to speak. Most people spend the time they should be listening preparing what they are going to say next, so how can they be listening? If you delay what you are going to say, maybe you'll find that it doesn't need to be said. Focus on the other person, and really be there. Don't worry about preparing to be brilliant.

3) Know the purpose of your listening. Are you listening to be amiable, to allow someone to vent, to find the customer's need, or to listen for who the person is? When you know which one it is, you will adjust accordingly, and you will be less ambivalent as a listener and more focused on serving the person.

4) Check on the accuracy of your listening by reflecting back to the other person. Instead of piping in with your contribution to the conversation, first reflect back something that lets the other person know you were really listening. You might say something like "So what you're saying is . . ." or "It sounds like . . ."

Listening is time well invested in the relationship, and as you practice this skill, you will become sharper and even more intuitive than before. You will start to see similarities in people, which will make you more sensitive and, therefore, more people-friendly. Being an expert about your own needs will make you that much more sensitive and accurate about other people's as well, lending even more power to your presentation. Your ease with people on the phone and in person is one of the biggest ingredients in your success. Never underestimate the power of the listener.

SERVICE

You've taken care of your needs, and you're becoming a better listener, which will take your selling to the next level. The next layer to add to this process is service. You must serve your clients so well that you make it a pleasure to buy from you. This starts when they become prospects and doesn't end when you've made the sale. If you think of each customer as a customer for life, you'll never stop serving them. What you're doing is servicing your future sales; if you do this, believe me, there will be future sales, many of them. It has to become an automatic way of being for you and yet requires a delicate balance between serving well and wasting your time. If you're serving the wrong person, like the person who is never going to buy, you are barking up the wrong tree and wasting your energy. Giving great service also means giving it to the right people. An ideal client profile will help (see chapter 5). Keener listening skills will help you recognize when you're speaking to an ideal client.

What do you do now to serve your customers? How could you do more? The simplest form of service includes such basics as keeping your word, being on time and respectful of clients' time, treating them with courtesy, and knowing your product or service well. This is not enough; it's minimal. Slowing the sales roller coaster will require extraordinary service, and the best part is that you don't have to knock yourself out to do it. Follow the five points below, and you'll be well on your way.

1) Become the expert. Know your product or service so thoroughly that you could win contests in your company for being in the know. You will be valuable to your prospects and customers when you can answer all their questions. This is great service.

2) Develop a reputation for being the best. This differs from being an expert, because it has a broader scope. First, know your product or service inside out, and second, let other people know that you're the one who knows. Make a commitment to be the best in your field. You want your clients and prospects to get the sense that they not only get the product, they also get you. Clients who feel that they got the best feel better served and better overall about their purchase.

Build that reputation by becoming very visible and by having extraordinary results or customers to build your reputation on. Success breeds success. One wonderful success builds into others. Tell stories of satisfied customers. As long as you're bragging about them and not you, it should not be offensive to anyone.

3) Share what you learn. Anything you have learned yourself about business, the news, sports, fashion, life, money, selling, or any topic under the sun that may be of interest to people is worth sharing. Something that is relevant to what your clients purchase from you, or something that interests them, is especially valuable.

4) Provide client extras. What can you do for your clients that is above and beyond the call of duty, but reasonable and acceptable and connected to what you are selling? Car salesmen may give away a free calendar that includes car maintenance reminders. Computer software salespeople may include training time with each purchase. I lead special seminars and teleclasses just for clients on topics that are of interest to them and that we can apply to our one-on-one calls. Print brokers may include personalized stationery for an office. This is not restricted, of course, to give-away items. It can be extra time spent educating clients on a product or helping them with another area of business that doesn't involve a sale. My real estate agent goes out of his way to keep me informed of what the other houses on my block are selling for, to keep me abreast of how my property value is going up. I love that he's taken the time although I did not ask him to do it. He's smart. I will use him when we are ready to move or refer him to anyone I know in the area. It's been a long time since we bought the house, and he hasn't stopped serving us.

5) Say thank you. Thank people for choosing you or buying from you; you'll leave your customer feeling great about doing business with you. Don't let the payment be the end of the transaction. As trivial as this may sound, one of the few things I hated about living in New York City was that the cashiers at the supermarket never said thank you. Even if I thanked them when I received my change, they never said a word. That was when I really understood how important it is to close the selling chapter of your relationship gracefully (or should I say, gratefully) and enter the next stage of service. Showing your appreciation is crucial to more sales. That goes for referrals too. Trace every one, and make sure you thank each referral source, even if the referral did not become a customer. It's good business, and great service.

OPERATING ON A FULL TANK

The final ingredient in getting the sales roller coaster to even out and to give you dependable success is the concept of operating on a full life tank, literally and figuratively having more than enough—more than enough money, time, customers, prospects, support, resources, friends, and so on, you name it— more than enough of everything you need. Having a full tank is a mental concept as well; you need a mental and emotional reserve so you are not running on empty. Having your needs met is one way to keep your tank full emotionally. If you ran your car on a near-empty gas tank, it would be puttering on fumes and would likely sputter to a halt. The same goes for you, your business, and your life. If you or your sales efforts are running on empty, the fumes will give you headaches, not to mention erratic results.

Getting your needs met and nurturing your prospects and clients should put you well on your way to keeping a full tank. Take a few moments to decide where else you will work to create reserves so that you are driving with a full tank. This will make you much more attractive to your customers. If they even sense that you are coming from need or desperation, it will affect your chances of closing the sale. Being "full" allows you a certain level of detachment that makes you very attractive to your client. Of course, you don't want to go too far and come off as arrogant. Even if your tank is not totally full yet, act as if it is, and you will start seeing the outside circumstances of your business change to match what you are dictating from the inside.

Feed your needs, but eat healthy.

Calm the Sales Roller Coaster

1. Identify your personal needs.
2. Get them met outside of work and get them out of your way.
3. Attract the customer to you.
4. Become a better listener by putting yourself in the client's shoes.
5. Learn to serve REALLY well.
6. Operate on a FULL life tank.
7. Enjoy a smooooooth ride.

EIGHT

Overqualified and Underutilized— Whose Fault Is It?

*"I know I'm better than most of the people
I work with. Why am I the last one to be
called into a project?"*

SCOTT, IN HIS EARLY THIRTIES, WAS A RECENT IVY LEAGUE MBA graduate who had been at his job at a large investment banking firm for almost two years when he came to work with me. He worked ridiculously long hours and lived for his annual bonus check, which was the only thing that kept him going. He felt that he was ignored for every project that could have meant something to his advancement and felt that the powers that be were not even aware of his existence. When it came time for semiannual reviews, he was pleased neither with what they had to say nor with his accomplishment.

Overworked and overtired, Scott started falling into a slump and began to feel sorry for himself. He resented anyone telling him what to do and was soon perceived as a problem employee.

He drew attention to himself in negative ways and alienated people by being uncooperative and autocratic. He felt that no one understood his frustration; he felt that he was highly qualified but was being asked to do things that were beneath him. His job was never threatened, but he was headed down the wrong path if he didn't change soon. It was time to get his act together. I warned him that if he wanted to become my client, he would have to be willing to go for it, and I wouldn't tolerate his whining. The sign over my desk does not read THOU SHALT NOT WHINE for nothing. He agreed, and we were ready for business.

First, Scott needed to have some semblance of a life. He had no time to recharge, which was not helping his performance at all. He started leaving the office at 5:30 or 6:30 when he wasn't under a deadline for a proposal, he began enjoying evenings with friends, and he got back to dating. He had always been concerned that he couldn't leave the office at a decent hour because he wouldn't be seen as a team player. How ironic; before we implemented this, he still wasn't being seen as a team player, even when he was putting in eighteen to twenty hours a day. Nonetheless, once he felt like a human again and not a droid, we had someplace to go to crank up his performance.

Scott needed to change the way he was perceived within his organization. I encouraged him to be very quiet about the changes we were about to make; there was no need to talk about them. The changes had to start showing for him to get noticed; indiscretion would not help him correct the damage that had already been done. I did, however, want him to start documenting everything that he thought he was doing a great job on, especially projects that could be brought up at review time.

Scott starting raising his standards. We analyzed what actions he could start taking that would be holding him to a higher ideal than the one he had been maintaining. For example, he held himself to a quicker response time in answering calls and e-mail. He also held himself to changing his communication style. He made a pact to start being supportive of everyone around him, regardless of rank or title. Before this, he had a tendency to use his MBA status to measure who would or would not be worth his time. He also devoted himself to learning much more about the services his company offered and to getting ahead of the curve in learning about the company's clients. None of this was required for his job, but it started getting him noticed. Scott needed to strengthen the professional relationships that would be beneficial to him within the company. He used to complain about being overlooked, yet he never went out of his way to come in contact with these people, so what did he expect?

Another element that became essential to improving Scott's performance was helping him develop an idea of where this position fit into a bigger picture for him. Applying some meaning to his job made it become more than a way to pay the rent and infused it with an excitement he could not find before. After we did some exploration, it was very clear that Scott wanted to have his own business, and he wanted to capitalize most of it himself. He wasn't sure exactly what he wanted to get into, but he was certain that his current position would give him the experience he would need to succeed and that if he played his cards right, he could earn and save a substantial amount of money for his new venture. Once he could see it, he was motivated to achieve it.

We worked together a total of eight months, which brought us to another semiannual review. He had succeeded; perception had changed. This was noted in his review, and he was also able to share the projects he could point to as his accomplishments. He was finally asked to lead projects in which he would be supervising other people. He was told that if he remained consistent, he would be relied on more and more. By his next review, his total salary, including bonuses, had jumped from just a little over $100,000 to double that. Since then, Scott's bonuses have kept going up. He has put away enough to do whatever he chooses. In the meanwhile, I assume he'll be busy planning his wedding. The last time we spoke, he reported great news at work and told me he was engaged to be married.

If you are finding yourself in this kind of situation, it can look pretty bleak from where you stand, but from over here, it's pretty simple. If you don't think you're being valued for what you can do, you have two choices: Get out or get moving. Your strengths may not be a match for your job, but I would probably rule that out nine times out of ten. It's more likely that you're waiting for someone to see all you can offer. No one is going to hand you the goods, sweetheart. If they can't see what's great about you, it's probably because you don't see it enough yourself. And if you are seeing it, you're not living it. So stop feeling sorry for yourself; you've got work to do.

It was once a concern for only the entry-level employee, but more and more of you are finding yourselves shuffled around in a company and having to prove yourselves to a new boss or new colleagues. This is no longer a once-in-a-career spot that people find themselves in; people today are changing positions more times in the span of their working life than ever before. They are often put into situations in which no one knows what they can do, so they are underutilized until their strengths become evident. That's where you come in. Stop hiding! Don't be afraid to get noticed. Get out there and shine! Modesty and waiting to get noticed never got you a date to the prom or picked for a sports team, and they're not going to get you a promotion either.

WHO YOU HAVE TO BE

Be somebody! Don't wait for someone else to deem you worthy, ready, able, or anything else; decide it for yourself. Even though circumstances might not allow you to do all you want to do right now, you have to change your attitude to change the circumstances more quickly. First and foremost is getting over yourself. I mean it. Be an adult. It's embarrassing when I have to say this to clients who are fifteen to twenty years older than I am. At this critical turning point, you just have to say, "Hell, I am what I am, and I'm going to make the best of it." You have to take the good with the bad in yourself. You are much stronger and more attractive if you honor what is underdeveloped in you than if you try to hide it or overcompensate for it. It's much more powerful to say, "I'm not sure of those numbers; I'll get back to you." Your alternatives are to make up an answer or to freeze like a deer caught in headlights. A degree of self-acceptance will ease your struggle in getting noticed on the job. Being frustrated and anxious about that stuff is just as futile as trying to get your needs met where they can't be met. Having your needs met comes into play here too. When you get over yourself, you take responsibility for finding solutions to your own frustrations instead of wallowing in them. Can you be that person? Here are a few things that will help:

1) **Raise your standards.** Expect more from yourself. Even if no one else expects more of you, do it for yourself. Just as your boundaries dictate what you will take from other people, your standards are the things that you hold yourself to, that tell people who you are and what you can be counted on to do. Just as Scott decided to raise his standard—returning calls quickly and delivering on what he promised—you can improve the way you do certain things. For example, you might show up early to every meeting instead of getting there just as it starts. You could stop engaging in office gossip, to upgrade the quality of your relationships. You may also be the first one to share your ideas instead of kicking yourself later because someone else mentioned them first. You get the idea. Look at your productivity level, the quality of the work you do, and how often you take initiative as the places where your standards can be raised. Clean up your work area, create new ways of doing the same old tasks, come up with solutions for department-wide problems, double-check your work to avoid errors, take a risk a week, or even raise the number of friendly exchanges you have. (Note: Standards can be too high. If keeping yourself to a new standard is causing you to suffer or beat yourself up, lower it immediately. The point is not to cause you to become a driven overachiever, but rather to raise the stakes so that you play a bigger game.)

Take a moment to note three standards you can raise right away that will make a difference.

2) **Invest in yourself.** Just as Scott started to learn more about his company's products and did additional research on its clients, you can invest in training yourself. Invest in your ability to do more, or learn something that can make you more

money down the road. Decide to be a master at what you do, even if your current position limits that. Prepare yourself now for being two levels ahead. Know your product really well. Learn about your industry and the competition. Be a pro. If you want to be treated as one of the best, take the initiative to become that. Make the time to do the professional reading that you always say you want to do. Ask your management to send you to a training program that interests you. Even if they don't, go anyway.

Invest in your wardrobe and outward appearance. This is a way to feel good about what you are putting forward, and it may get you noticed. While we're dealing with externals, you may consider taking a few sessions with a presentation skill coach to spruce up the way you present yourself. The bottom line is to invest in yourself because you are worth it. You will show up differently when you treat yourself better.

3) Decide what you want to be known for. If you can narrow in on what matters to you most and where you want to have the greatest impact, you will give yourself a good frame of reference for the actions you take. Do you want to make a difference in policy? Do you want to make a difference with people? Do you have a vision for your industry that excites you? Do you care about systems and how things get done? Listen to your instincts about what matters to you, and refocus some of your efforts there. Maybe you think that you can't make a difference at your current status, even if you pick one of these things. I see it differently. We want you to stand out and be put on a track to use all that you are capable of; this happens to people who have strong opinions that contribute to the bigger picture of an organization. Right? Right! So be that person. Have an opinion.

You do want to stay with the current to a certain degree instead of fighting it, but don't be afraid to have a pet project that matters to you.

A client who had just been placed in a new management position, and who very much wanted to make her mark quickly, decided that having an impact on each person she came in contact with was what she wanted to be known for. She called it her personal marketing campaign. She was supportive yet firm, and she concentrated on always being able to really pay attention to people when they spoke. She helped a lot of people both below and above her do their jobs better. She made a very quick and smooth transition, one that I think this focus made possible.

Promise me, however, that you won't choose to be known for being a nice guy/great girl. By all means, be a great human people want to work with, but please don't make it your be-all and end-all. It may sound noble, but that is a load of baloney. This will only keep you exactly where you are—feeling like you can do so much and wondering why no one is noticing. They are too busy using you and seeing how much they can get away with, that's why. Choose wisely and yes, be liked, but don't make it your goal.

WHAT YOU HAVE TO DO

The internal shifts you've made in attitude and style should be starting to work, but you'll need to do a few more things to get you to where you want to be. If you're serious about being recognized for what you can do, you'll need to help people see it. Here's how:

1) Document your accomplishments. Scott kept a record of the number of projects he had done and the major contributions he made to them. You'll need to keep a quantifiable record of what you have accomplished. Did something you do save the company money? Did you complete a record number of projects in a given time? Did you innovate an idea that got implemented to great effect? Were you responsible for x amount of people getting trained in something? Look for important, measurable accomplishments that you can compile and present when it's time for your performance review. Don't assume that the people who make the decisions know that you did these things. They may notice certain improvements or one big thing that occurred, but when you can present a fact sheet, it has a much more powerful impact. Scott's bonuses were decided as a result of this kind of presentation.

2) Give up competing and start collaborating. In the eagerness to get ahead, you may fall into the very human trap of competing with the perceived threats to your advancement. We all know there are some pretty nasty people out there, but if you can't get away from them, work with them instead of against them. Collaborate on projects and make yourself valuable to their process. It will demystify you and work greatly in your favor, correcting misperceptions about you. You will be embodying the spirit of a team player as well as getting a chance to show your stuff. Letting any animosity fester will never prove productive or get you positive attention, no matter how right you think you are to feel the way you do. We treat our perceptions as reality, but once we take a closer look, we may find that our assumptions were wrong. Be open to that as you collaborate with your competitors, and watch them open up to you as their assumptions melt away too.

3) Stop apologizing or making excuses. If you are feeling overqualified and underutilized, you probably find yourself eager to defend any situation in which misperception about you could be turned further against you. If you find yourself getting defensive or explaining yourself a lot, stop. You are just digging the hole even deeper. Take responsibility; you will make a stronger impact if you find a solution to a negative situation rather than talking about why it's not your fault or about how you might have done it differently. Just do it, and you'll make your point. Show, don't tell—no reason, no justification. Just make the changes that are needed. Acknowledge mistakes; don't hide it if you're not going to make a deadline; tell the truth. Excuses only cheat you of the reputation as a mover and an achiever that you have been craving.

4) Check in with your reality checker. Develop a good relationship with somebody in the organization who can become a reality-checker for you, someone who really knows the situations you face and can give you independent feedback about your take on things. This could also be someone outside the company, but it has to be someone objective who will not automatically take your side, somebody who can really listen and hear through your slant on things to measure where you are off base or where you are right on with your assumptions. This person should ground you in reality and help you make smart strategic decisions, serving as a fair, objective sounding board who wants the best for you and can keep anything you say in strict confidence. Give yourself the gift of sharing the burden. There is no need to feel isolated; it only makes matters worse.

*　　*　　*

Christine, a fifty-year-old sales and marketing specialist, came to work with me shortly after joining a management consulting firm that turned her down as a partner, but still valued her enough to want her on its team. She was working in a research and support capacity, more than an administrative assistant but not at the partner level where she wanted to be. She was turned down for that level because it was thought that she lacked the contacts and connections to bring in a substantial amount of business to the firm. It was also a career change for her, and her potential was not recognized by the company. She agreed to take the job to learn this new field better, not anticipating how resentful she would feel when other partners, who were candidates no stronger than she was, were later added to the firm.

Our first job was to get her over her learning curve as fast as possible. The partners were right in thinking that she did not know the business well enough to be at the top level. She found it hard to be patient during that time, but once she was over the hump, in about four or five months, we were able to take action to make her partnership material. Before it would become easy, there was still one more obstacle in the way: She was still resentful of her situation and wanted to spend our sessions talking about how unfair it was. I said that we had to be proactive, or forget it. She agreed with me, and off she went. As she worked for the partners, she began to take time to make contacts of her own. She started to network, finding her way to people who would consider her and the firm for their consulting needs.

Meanwhile, as she shed her poor-me stance, her relationship with the partners started to change. They began giving her more independent assignments that did not require their approval or supervision. She also stopped competing with the newer partners whom she had perceived as threats. She asked to join them on a few of their projects, which strengthened her relationships with them, but also taught her more about the business than she would have learned otherwise. As we wrapped up our work together, we were exploring whether or not staying with her current firm was really her best option. Her situation had improved significantly, and all her networking had led to offers at other firms that were ready to consider her for the level she wanted. Giving up the battle and finally taking responsibility for her situation paid off. She now had the wonderful dilemma of having too many good opportunities to choose from.

COMMUNICATION AND RELATIONSHIPS

There are two themes that emerge as we explore building a positive internal reputation and making sure you are noticed for all you can do. These central elements are communication and relationships. Without a flow of communication, your ability to influence others' perceptions of you will be limited. As your contact points for communication, relationships will become very important. It's critical that you learn how to build them. Where do you fall short here? Are you isolating yourself in reaction to feeling unrecognized? Do you avoid sharing your opinion or dealing with conflict? Do you shy away from taking more responsibility?

You now have the opportunity to forge relationships where you didn't have the chance before. Stronger relationships will not come from schmoozing. People know when they are being buttered up or courted. Instead, you'll make an impact by getting involved and having access to people you wouldn't normally meet. You will need to do more than show up and shake hands, however. You'll need to share your opinion or be ready to take action. Having the guts to introduce yourself to the president or chairman every chance you get won't do it, but writing him or her a letter with your ideas that might contribute to the bigger picture might. Gutsy, huh?

If you're serious about pulling yourself out of the rut you're in, you'll have to turn strangers into fans. You will need to network internally and externally. Get involved in professional groups in which you will both learn more about your industry and how to advance in it and meet people with whom you can build goodwill. These outside contacts are just as important as your relationships inside the company, because they might know some of the very people who need to hear good things about you in order to become fans. There is nothing like a nod from a peer to make someone else question their judgment of you. Getting involved is equally important to networking. People won't really get a chance to meet you unless they've had a chance to work alongside you or to discuss important matters with you. Volunteer to be on a task force or committee or an extra project. Don't spread yourself too thin, but do put yourself out there.

Ideally, seeking out a mentor in your company would be a great way to link you to the organization. Mentors are hard to find these days because of the constant reshuffling of people and time constraints, but it is not impossible to find them. This kind of relationship will result from your sticking your neck out and asking someone to take on that role for you. Make sure it is someone who is accessible and who has already demonstrated some level of rapport with you. A mentor can help you learn more about your company, your industry, and what you might expect for your career path. Most important, a mentor can be an advocate. The vote of approval from someone at a more senior level than you could influence those who are closer to you on a daily basis but who have yet to fully appreciate you.

Now that you have established some contact points inside and outside the organization, the way you communicate with these people is going to make the difference. Remember: We want there to be a flow of communication, and your relationships are the vehicle for that. The way you relate to people, whether or not they are your fans, will make the difference. If you are battling a negative perception of you, your one-on-one communication will be your only proving ground. Your style will reflect what comes back to you. Here are a couple of suggestions for keeping the lines of communication open and fostering better workplace relationships.

1) Be a model. Keep your awareness level high enough so that you can communicate with people in the way that you would like them to speak to you. If the coffee room chitchat is useless gossip, don't join in to be part of the crowd. Be constructive, and lead the conversation in a more positive direction. Use your boundaries to keep away the content and tone of conversations that you don't want to participate in. As long as you are not critical of people and are always constructive, even in requesting a change in tone or behavior, communication will be smoother. Even if you have to respond to an irate boss, just remember to hold your ground. Model the communication style you want people to have with you by using it with them.

2) Make people right. Even if the irate boss is yelling at you, make the boss right. Say, "You have every reason to feel that way." "I can understand why you are upset." "I'd feel the same way in your position." This is not to position you as a boss-fearing yes-man (or -woman). Nor should you compromise yourself and let someone abuse you or walk all over you. If you formally acknowledge others' points of view, you will smooth the flow of communication so you can be heard. If you fight or make excuses, you will shut down the lines of communication, and they will think you're in the wrong on whatever issue they are upset about. If they can be made right instead of being fought with, you just may get a chance to set the conversation on a better course and come to a resolution on the matter at hand.

Think of it this way: Even if people are wrong, they are right, because they are coming from the limit of their own growth and experience. They cannot do better, or else they would be doing better in that moment. So for that moment, even if you want to correct them, they are right. By letting that be so, you have kept the flow of communication open.

A customer walks into a bank in an uproar because his statement incorrectly shows that he has bounced a check, and he was charged $20 for it for the second time in a row. He demands to see the manager and proceeds to rant and rave about his situation. The manager has two choices: He can start fighting with the customer, or he can make him right. If he's good at customer service, he will say, "Mr. Jones, you have every reason to be upset; let's see what we can do about this." By making Mr. Jones right, he will probably be able to move on to a solution rather quickly. If he had not made him right, he would likely have lost a customer. Now what does this have to do with you? If you treat each person in your organization as a customer, you will have much smoother sailing. I am not intimating that you should take abuse; rather, you should use this as a way to promote more rational conversation when there is a problem, and better communication overall when there is no problem.

3) **Manage up.** A great way to increase the flow of communication between you and your boss or manager is to manage up. That means telling your manager how to help you do a great job, telling him or her how to help you succeed. Britt, the VP who got promoted to national director, used this as a way to improve her relationship with her boss. It was the deeper level of contact and communication with him that led to her promotion. Her request of him was simple, but it had a great impact, far greater than she would ever have imagined. She simply asked that they be in communication more often as a way to help her be able to do a great job. They created a system of e-mail and personal meetings that cemented their relationship and obviously gave him enough contact to become very impressed with her. He even decided to manage up to his superiors himself, even though he didn't know to call it that. Don't be afraid to get what you need from your boss to do a great job. If you think hiding it presents a stronger image, you're wrong. Asking for support and opening up that channel of communication can only be beneficial.

The secret to moving from feeling overqualified and underutilized to feeling that you have license to contribute as fully as you can is to stop suffering over what *could* be and start getting it *to* be, now. Your present is the best investment you can make in your future. We've explored many ways for you to get noticed for what you can really do; you need to look at this from a whole other angle. You need to take control of your own career and make it what you want it to be. Don't let circumstances dictate it for you. If you start thinking like an entrepreneur, you'll start to get this. You no longer work for a company; you work for yourself. Instead of building a business, you're building a career step-by-step, adding the skills and credentials you feel you need to get you where you want to go. Scott did just that. He stayed where he thought he would learn what he needed to know to run his own enterprise. Christine did that too. She knew it wasn't the perfect situation, but she got what she needed from it to catapult her to the next step.

Have a plan. You have to build your own career and résumé; no one will do it for you. If it seems that a situation is not allowing you to shine, *you* are not allowing yourself to shine. Get in touch with why you are where you are in the first place. If it's not the right place, find another. If you feel it's the right place to be, do all you can to be the kind of person who doesn't need to manipulate and scheme to be seen. Have an impact on others through the actions you take and the way you take them. Others will notice; you won't have to point it out.

Stop hiding, and start shining!

Go from Feeling Overqualified and Underutilized to Fully Contributing

▼

1. Stop feeling sorry for yourself; get over yourself.
2. Raise your standards; show people who they are dealing with.
3. Invest in yourself.

4. Stop competing, and start collaborating.
5. Document your accomplishments. You need to see them, and others do too.
6. Turn strangers into fans by networking and mentoring.
7. Improve the flow of communication.
8. Be responsible for your own career.
9. Enjoy being a STAR!

NINE

The Hero Syndrome—
A Manager's Downfall,
a Coach's Dream

"I'm so busy managing everything that comes at me
from my staff that I don't have any time to do my
own work, much less get home at a decent hour."

EORGE, A SENIOR MANAGER IN HIS EARLY FORTIES, WAS WORKING
for a highly visible technology firm when he hired me to
help him become a more effective manager. He did not lack experience by any means, but he did feel like he was on an endless
backslide as he tried to navigate his organization forward.
Problems were never-ending, and he never seemed to have
enough hours in the day to complete everything that he had to
do. His stress level was astronomical, and he worked so many
hours that he could hardly keep track of what day it was. On
top of that, he had an uncooperative staff because he had lost
their trust and respect. Everything he had tried to turn things

down a more positive path had failed, and he knew he had to do something. What finally drove him to call me was his latest performance review, which included a 360-degree feedback survey of him by everyone in his organization. The picture was bleak, but he was given the chance to redeem himself.

When we took a look at all the circumstances George was putting up with, it became clear that he had to change before he could see if there was any chance of his organization functioning better. Contrary to what you might think, the problem was not that he had an autocratic style that was off-putting to his people. It was actually that he was too "nice," and he commanded no respect from them. At first it seemed like he was the greatest guy because he pounced on any problem and relieved others' responsibility for it, but over time, this started to work against him. His people became resentful that he could not solve their problems because he had taken on so many that he couldn't keep his promises about any of them. Furthermore, I felt they were becoming restless and bored because they had no challenges to overcome. He took care of all the challenges for them.

The best things about George were that he never lost his sense of humor, and he was very open to feedback about himself that could be helpful. When I told him that I thought he was suffering from Hero Syndrome, he could chuckle and knew exactly what I meant. He had tried unsuccessfully to save the day, and it was time to get down to business. George called a meeting to announce that he would be doing things differently from now on, and that if anyone had any concerns or questions about those changes, he was available to discuss them. He scheduled individual meetings with each person, in which he clearly laid out exactly what was expected of them, and he set clear goals and parameters for those goals. We worked on a few problem-solving formulas, which he began to use with his staff, to teach them how to solve their own problems. He started to find himself with more time and was able to roam the halls and get a chance to see what was going on in his own organization. He started giving a lot more feedback as he saw things go well or go wrong.

Within six months, he had done it; he had turned the situation around. People wanted focus and structure, and he was now giving it to them. He was much more direct and firm, and he stopped trying to please everyone, which made him much more popular in the end. People knew he would not tolerate many of the negative things he had tolerated before, so over time those behaviors disappeared. People had confidence in him again, and that boosted their confidence in themselves. George had stopped managing and started coaching. He looked for the best in each person, and he insisted that they use it. He always had it in him, but he just didn't realize that he had stopped motivating others to perform and had taken the whole department on his shoulders. When he was first awarded the position, he fell into the trap of wanting to be liked, which led him away from his best management practices. Now that he had turned things around, he knew it would never happen again. His next review was excellent, and performance in his group had gone way up; he now had time for a weekly golf game and for quality time with his family.

You're such a great person. You're sooo nice, but look at the number you've done on yourself. You wanted to be liked; you wanted to save the day. Ouch! If you're so good, how could things be going so badly? You took your eye off the ball. You tried to get your personal needs met where you shouldn't have. Before it's too late, you're going to have to reclaim your position as manager. People need you to guide the way, to be the marker that gives them an idea of how they are doing, but after that, there isn't much they need you for. Sounds easy, huh? It is! That's the whole point.

Managing is burdensome. You have to track each task, follow up with people, and move the process along. It would be better to take on the latest coaching skills, which many managers are assimilating in these times of constant change. When you coach, you use a light touch. You make agreements up front about how things need to go. You agree on the circumstances if they don't go that way. You look for where people are doing great instead of where they are screwing up. You demand excellence in a way that makes everyone want to attain it. It's a style of communicating that you can easily adopt to free yourself up to have more time and a more effective operation. People want to be used to their fullest potential. If you change your style and adjust where you put your attention, you can do just that, and you'll be manager of the year. Coaching skills can really make the difference.

Oh, wait. Before we go any further, I want to make sure that you haven't conjured up the image of a football coach on the sidelines yelling at his team in order to motivate them. The sports coach is in the same family as the manager-as-coach, but there is no yelling involved. You must develop a way to become an even-keeled, direct, yet nonthreatening manager who commands respect. Anger and tantrums are excluded. It's a delicate balance, but one you can reach if you put your mind to it.

Cynthia was a new manager who had a tendency to lose her cool. It was really hard for her to hide when she was angry about something. She would try to remain calm when she talked to people, but you could see the anger in her face as she gritted her teeth and held back a sarcastic tone. She had the fortunate/unfortunate situation of being a smart and quick woman who did not have the patience to wait for other people to see what she saw. When she committed to work on her management skills with me, she knew this would be one of the first things we had to turn around.

Our first job was to get the angry charge out of her voice, to help her find a way to use *what* she said to express her frustration instead of dramatizing it in *how* she said it. Thomas Leonard calls this "charge neutral." With charge neutral, you can say anything to anyone, even if it is not positive, in such a way that they can hear it without an angry reaction. As one of my colleagues once said, "It's like sipping a mint julep on the veranda on a warm summer day," laid back, yet very effective and refreshing. Cynthia learned to say things like, "I am frustrated by how many times we have gone over this," without losing her cool. Communicating with her staff and getting the results she wanted came so much more easily when she was perceived as fair and firm instead of volatile. Unfortunately, angry women are perceived as bitches, while men seem to get away with it more easily. Nonetheless, charge neutral will do wonders for both sexes in getting their message heard.

What Cynthia was doing, and what George came to do as well, was to become a model for the people they worked with. They modeled behavior, attitude, and standards that people couldn't help but start to emulate. They had no choice but to emulate them, because these managers accepted nothing less. They were challenging them to be more, which in turn caused them to do things more effectively. This was only possible, though, when the managers could model this behavior. If they couldn't do those things themselves, it was harder to get other people to do so. This is the challenge you are presented with. Master the skills in this chapter and you'll be a powerful model, eliciting powerful behavior from others.

As we outline the changes you will have to make to take on this latest management style, the most important thing to understand is that you are going to stop managing tasks and start coaching people. It will yield you even better results with less effort on your part. When you find yourself with too much time on your hands, you'll know you succeeded.

YOUR NEW JOB DESCRIPTION

When it comes to dealing with the people in your organization or business, there are only four possible things you will be doing with your time: You will be spelling out goals and expectations, teaching them how to solve their own problems, endorsing them, and pointing out where they need to improve. That's it. There will be no need for long meetings, chasing information, or monitoring their every move; those days are gone. So let's take a look at each of these parts of your new job description to make sure that you never do things the old way again.

Goals and Expectations—Mapping

Mapping requires spelling out each person's journey toward the mission of the organization. They need to understand their destination, the time you expect them to arrive at their destination, what awaits them if they don't get there in time, and what landmarks and guideposts to look for along the way. It's up to them to choose which route they want to take to get there, but there should be no doubt about what you expect from them. This will save you countless hours of backtracking and chasing results. You are both in agreement on what has to happen and what will occur if it doesn't happen. When you coach them, you must trust them to find their own answers once the parameters are set.

Teaching Others How to Solve Problems

You will want to guide people through this process the first couple of times. As you do so, you will be modeling for them how to do it when you are not around. Teach them that you are not a problem-solving machine and that you expect them to do it themselves. When you coach them, you believe in the better part of them that can do that. Here is your script:

What have you tried?
What haven't you tried?
What will get you the result you want?
What is your plan?
Who can help you and how?
How will you know if you have succeeded?

Refuse to get sucked into problems. Don't hand-hold. Don't let people waste your time. Yes, be compassionate and constructive, but make the investment in solutions and not in problems. For example, the staff member of a manager who was trying this out came to her and asked her to review something he had written. The manager asked him if he was happy with what he had written. The staff person said he hadn't really looked at it too closely. The manager said: "When you've reviewed it and are happy with it, I'll be glad to take a look at it."

Endorsing

The word "you" needs to become the most commonly used word in your vocabulary. Right now, "I" is. Start going out of your way to find things to endorse in people. Point out something they've done well. Point out positive traits about them. Give them extra attention when they are stretching beyond their comfort zone. Just endorse, endorse, endorse. Are they doing good work? Have they effected a great change? Point it out, all of it. Don't respond only when they've made a mistake. Success breeds success. Let them know what is great, and they will do more of it. That's coaching.

Correcting Behavior

Separate the behavior from the person, and you'll never dread a confrontation again. Whenever there has been a mistake or something is going south, don't wait to see how it plays out or wait until next time to do something about it. Make your staff aware of what you know as soon as you know it, even if it seems minor at the time. If you let things add up, you will be resentful or even inappropriately blow your top later on when you can't stand it anymore. When you do have to address mistakes and problems, endorse the person and correct only the behavior that you need to correct. Keep the person whole, and be very specific about the problem and you will find people less defensive, more able to take criticism, and ready to bounce back to full performance more quickly than if you used a personal attack along with pointing out what was done wrong. Remember that, as their coach, you are *for* them, not against them. Your own needs are taken care of, so you don't have to be right or superior to feel good about yourself.

Fine-Tuning

You'll need to fine-tune your people skills until management is a hands-off kind of discipline for you. You'll need to develop a keen sense of people beyond what you already have, and learn how to nurture their performance without a great deal of cost to you. The time you spend giving of yourself as a manager/ coach will pay off; you will have more time to handle your own tasks, and time to fill as you please. Fine-tuning your skills will be worth the time you invest in the returns you will receive in the form of your staff's success, your own, and the freedom you will experience. George became known as someone to whom people could come to learn more about themselves and how to do their best, but no one ever expected him to take care of them. They were not dumping their problems on him; they knew he was best at getting them to see their way to succeeding on their own.

Telling the Truth

We've talked about this in different ways throughout this book, but to a manager it has its own special meaning. Many clients will tell me the truth about an employee, a colleague, or a situation and then proceed to tell me about a scheme or plan to skirt the issue and somehow still get the desired result. My response is the same: "Just tell the truth."

Why is that not the first choice? I know you often do this at home as well as in the office. The truth is the fastest route to a solution. If you are lacking the right words to deliver the truth, try this: Write down any unadulterated truth that comes to mind even if it comes out in a horrible, damaging way. Next, once you can see on paper what is at the core of the issue for you, look for the language to express it in a way that will allow the message to be heard without becoming inflammatory. Without this short process, you're usually tempted to omit or manipulate the truth, because the way it comes to mind is too harsh to say to anyone. No problem. Just write down the truth and then put it in terms someone can relate to as positive guidance for change.

Orientation

You'll have to get good at orienting people to their own growth. Think about a time when you were asked to stretch beyond what you really thought you could do, but you were willing to give it a try. You were probably a combination of confidence and nerves and perhaps even had bouts of losing that confidence altogether. If someone had told you that you would probably experience that combination of emotions and circumstances, wouldn't it have been easier to get through? If someone had done that for you, you could have had an orientation to familiarize yourself with the process and, as a result, demystify what you were about to go through. You wouldn't have felt alone, wrong, dumb, or too embarrassed to ask for more help. If you start doing this for people, you'll be saving them time and angst. They will be less afraid to strive for bigger goals because they'll know what to expect. You will create a context in which they can measure their own growth. Tell people what to expect when you ask them to reach beyond what they have done before. You're not their caretaker if you do this; you are simply shining a light on an unknown path, saving them time and struggle.

In coaching one client to tell the truth to someone on his team, I oriented him to the possibility that coming straight out with the truth when he wasn't used to doing that could cause him to create a mess that he would have to clean up afterward if the conversation did not go smoothly. When he had an idea of what could backfire, he became determined to not let that happen and gave thoughtful consideration to preparing for that conversation. It went well and all ended peacefully, but his orientation caused him to perform better than he might have if he hadn't known what to expect.

Making Requests

Part of your job is asking people to do things. There is something even more powerful about making very big requests of the people who work with you. There is a difference between just asking and making a request. Asking is nice, and it sounds optional. Making a request is more a directive, and it has a non-threatening challenge to it that people respond to. "I request that you put this skill into effect immediately" is more powerful than "Let me ask you to start using this right away." People are just waiting for you to ask a lot of them. When you ask them to stretch, they surprise even themselves.

Be careful to keep an angry or forceful tone out of any request. That would turn it into a threat or demand. A very big request can be made firmly without being a threat.

Connecting

Take the time to connect with people. People are sick of being humored and heard on a surface level. It keeps them from being their best, because they don't feel they are being seen for who they are and what they can do. When you really connect with people, they feel that you really get them, which opens them up to building greater trust in their relationships with you. To make that connection, you'll need to stand in others' shoes, to understand them at any given moment. If you can connect with how hard something is, or even how great something is for them, you can demonstrate a level of understanding that shows that you hear and accept them. You might say something like "That tested you, didn't it?" or "You liked being out in front, didn't you?" or "That was harder than you expected it to be." This degree of understanding is fertile ground for introducing change or challenging them to go to the next level. It will help cement the relationship that can facilitate the results you are looking for.

Listening

Here we are, listening again. We just covered this in chapter 7 as we talked about salespeople listening to their customers. As the manager/coach, you will be listening to the people you need to draw great things from. We will take your listening ability to its next stage of development. As you listen to your team complain, explain, plan, or communicate with you in any other way, instant reactions probably come into your head, for instance, your next comment or question. In fine-tuning your listening, you'll want to start listening for clues to who people are instead of just the details of what they are saying. By listening for these clues, you will come to understand how to coach them to be their best. Listen beyond the problem they are describing; find out what caused the problem in the first place.

Instant Reactions	Listening for Clues
Why?	What's missing—skills, language, support?
How?	Strengths—are they using them?
Does this make sense?	Motivation—where will it come from?
Do I agree/disagree?	Language—are they saying what they mean to say?
Do I like/dislike this?	Needs—are they in the way?
Is this right/wrong?	Values—are they being honored?
Is this good/bad?	Personal or professional development—what's needed?
Can I connect this to what I know?	Behavior—is it new for them?

It takes great concentration to listen like this, but you can see that you will rise above managing and really effect changes that will enhance performance. Don't try to play God or be superhuman in adopting this style. I'm not asking you to play shrink either, but increasing your insight into yourself and people in general will help you uncover how you can manage people in a way that will produce great results without taxing you. People want to do well for you, but it will take your challenge, vision, and knowing how to get the best from them to do so.

As George developed his new style as a manager, we came up against a situation that gave him a perfect opportunity to use his new skills. One of his managers was bucking George's authority, becoming very uncooperative in meetings, and adopting a negative attitude that was catching on in the department. George had reprimanded this person before, but the behavior kept recurring. The next step might have been to escort him out the door, but the last conversation they had coincided with George's learning how he could listen better. It occurred to him that when he listened for more than the surface, he found that his manager was not using his strengths to their fullest. He was bucking authority because he wanted more authority himself. Of course, George wasn't going to give it to him just because he was having temper tantrums. Instead, he shared what he felt was the problem and mapped out goals and expectations for this manager that eventually would be rewarded with more authority and leadership responsibilities. By listening for clues instead of having instant reactions, George had found the key to turning his manager around.

Once you master your new job description and the skills you need to fine-tune, you will be doing an about-face, away from the heavy responsibility of doing and being it all for everyone in your charge. You can do better. You can show them how to be that for themselves. It's ultimately their responsibility; they are just waiting for you to show them how.

If you're managing, you're working too hard.

Go from Managing to Being the Manager-as-Coach

▼

1. Be a model.
2. Take the charge out of your voice.
3. Stick to your new job description (mapping, teaching problem solving, endorsing and correcting behavior).
4. Fine-tune your people skills.
5. Listen for clues as to what hinders others' performance.
6. Welcome aboard, Coach!

TEN

Having an Identity Crisis—It's Happening to the Best of Us

"I can't do THAT!"

TOM WAS AN EXECUTIVE FOR MANY YEARS AND HAD HIS MOST RE-cent stint at a huge financial corporation. In the midst of a large restructuring, he suddenly found himself unemployed. Being in his fifties in murky financial times did not make for an easy or even successful job search. As his confidence (and bank account) started to wane, he got an unusual opportunity. The local fish market owner in his small town, once an executive himself, asked if Tom would be interested in buying his business.

Tom wrestled with the decision whether or not to buy the business. Sure, there were financial concerns of making the investment, but the hardest part to reconcile was about identity. Who was he? Was he an executive? Could he be the local "fishmonger"? Was he white collar? Blue collar? Could he be a small business owner? What did it *mean* if his family had to buy a smaller house to support the transition?

In rallying his family and getting their input, Tom began to see that his wife and kids did not care about any identity attached to him or what that identity provided for them. They saw an opportunity for their dad to be happy, a way to keep him from being away on business travel (which had been a huge part of the time), and a chance at happiness as a family unit. They let go of the big house where the kids had all grown up with relative ease as Tom put his finance and business training to work to make the numbers gel. They all got through it fine as soon as Tom reconciled the changes in his "identity" for himself.

He is now the proud owner and local "great guy" of the town's fish market. One of his customers told me that he'd never shopped at the store before and now he would never dream of buying his fish anywhere else.

"Tom is a wonderful human being and I go in to see him six or seven times a week on my way back and forth to the train station across the street from his store," he said.

Tom recognized that he was a good man who prides himself on doing the "right thing" and, therefore, saw the business as a way to do the right thing for himself and his family. He also prides himself on running his business with great integrity in an industry that does not always operate that way. He is happy and he is a present dad, which to his family is worth more than anything.

Working with people in today's world where many need to reinvent their work life completely or where many deal with nontraditional roles between spouses or partners, it has become necessary to break free of an ingrained identity in order for change to happen. It is really hard to change or even to know what to change when you have an inflexible self-image or a strong self-identification that blinds you to opportunity.

Social conventions and how we are brought up to measure our worth came into play in Tom's decision like it does for many people. Shame or fear of being ashamed becomes an overriding emotion and one that should signal fabricated nonsense right away. Nonetheless, it can be crippling and keep you from what would make you happy and successful, so it needs to be dealt with. For some, counseling may even be required to get to the root of it.

Identity as a deciding factor in one's life is a problem for both men and women as the times demand more and more changes that break with previous social history. One woman in three outearns her spouse right now, thereby challenging conventional roles and mores. More men are running households, more women are the main breadwinner, and more people have to reinvent their lives entirely. For some, retirement has come before they were ready, and others have just felt it was time for some soul-searching. Of course, as a coach, I see this as a good thing. Coaches have always been about putting happiness and wholeness ahead of money and egocentric gains. The fun part is that this challenge to our identities is not a temporary phase. It is what will be required to succeed in the twenty-first century. If we do not allow this reorientation to occur, we will have more "stuck" folks who may be jobless out of their own stubbornness and resistance to change.

More and more people are faced with not only the loss of a job but perhaps the loss of an industry that got shipped abroad or one that has become a dinosaur and is now dispensable. How can you adapt and find work if you identify yourself solely by what you have done for years or what you have invested your life in as a course of study, vocation, and occupation? The bottom line is that the inner identity has to change. How you see yourself must change and then the outside circumstances will ease up for you. When you see yourself as a human being first—one that has a contribution to make that adds up to good—the opportunities will come.

Let's explore some of the ways that people are challenged when their self-concept is not keeping up with the pace of the outside world's demands.

FINANCE-BASED IDENTITY

Some people identify themselves by their income bracket. It may be their lifestyle that they are particularly aligned with, or maybe their self-concept is rooted in how others see them or behave toward them because of their financial status. Nonetheless, their identity is confirmed by their financial status. In the case of a job loss or other sudden loss of income, the individual will be tested in his resiliency. Sure, there may be money in the bank to rely on and contacts to tap for other possible employment. However, if this individual is not set up financially to support a forced retirement or semi-retirement, and a change has to happen, having a money-based identity may make change a greater challenge than it already is.

It is not fair to say that this would be true for everyone in this kind of position or that a money identity issue concerns only the wealthy. I recently worked with a man who was always gainfully employed until the last couple of years. He could not catch a break when it came to getting back into the computer field he was let go from. As he grew more frustrated, he understood that he had no choice but to consider other options and professions. Before he came to me, he had begun dabbling in the field of recruiting, but it seemed to be a temporary measure. As we worked on a list of other possibilities, the role of teacher kept showing up, but my client would vehemently react to the thought of it by griping about how little money one makes in that field. The weeks and months went by and he resolved to make his recruiting business a success. He did have the contacts to make a go of it and he did begin to make placements and make some money.

Even as he saw hope that he could make money in his new business, he kept feeling the teacher idea gnawing at him. He felt it was something he could be good at and enjoy, but again, he could not see himself as a teacher because he could not see himself at that income level. More significant, perhaps, was that his biggest fear wasn't really about his own financial health. His biggest concern was what people would say about him if he took this new step.

"What would you say if your ten-year-old daughter came to you worried about what her classmates were thinking of her?" I asked, knowing full well what the answer would be.

"I know, I know," he said.

Hey, I have no beef with him not wanting to make less money, that is his prerogative, but he knew he would be well suited to teaching and eventually even said he could see himself loving it. He did not love recruiting. Why put off happiness? Why not take action and see what happens? It is my experience that pursuing a path that has been put in your way that excites you often leads to unexpected surprises both monetarily and opportunity-wise, IF you can adjust your identity and self-concept. As time went on this client kept trying on the teacher identity for size and he began to take steps toward entering the field. The final outcome is yet to be determined.

PROFESSIONAL IDENTITY

Another way that we make it difficult to change or to accept change, for that matter, is by tethering ourselves to a professional identity. For example, if you identify yourself as a doctor or an artist or a journalist, you may have a prescribed set of parameters that limits your choices of behavior, habits, or even future endeavors. You feel that you are expected to behave a certain way that is congruent to being a certain kind of professional. For many artists, especially, what they will or will not do to support their art, even if they are struggling, comes under severe scrutiny and is only acted upon if it is perceived as something an artist would do.

As an example, I can offer you Ginny's story. She was an artist. She acted, painted, designed jewelry and clothes, and dabbled in the music business. She never made much money at any of her pursuits, but somehow she got by financially. When she hit a particularly difficult period, she refused all her family's and friends' suggestions and help in finding a job. Her reply: "An artist wouldn't do that." Yes, perhaps an artist who was paying the rent would not have to do that, but one who isn't may need to consider giving it a try. What resulted was a long stint on public assistance followed by a threat of eviction from her apartment. The identity of "artist" was so firm that in this case it came with its own set of rules and they worked against her.

The previous story is a dramatic example, but the point still holds firm for more mainstream professionals. If we are seeing ourselves through the lens of a certain profession, we can limit our choices when faced with a need for a change. If you think you are supposed to act a certain way or can do only certain things, you are limiting your capacity for satisfaction. How many times have you thought, "Oh, someone in my position can't do that"?

This reminds me of someone else who had at one time considered becoming a teacher. Daphne was a twenty-three-year-old woman about to graduate from college with a degree in mathematics who I was asked to coach for a television show. She was not sure what she wanted to do after college and was in a bit of a rush to figure it out since graduation was just around the corner. As she ran off her list of possible career choices, she mentioned being a teacher, but only as a notion she had already dismissed.

"I don't want to be just a teacher," she said.

"What does 'just' a teacher mean?" I asked curiously.

"Just a teacher. I'd be *just* a teacher," she replied.

"What's wrong with being a teacher?"

"I always thought I'd do something huge and that's not huge," Daphne said with her voice beginning to quaver.

"What kind of impact can a great teacher make?" I asked, expecting Daphne to surprise herself when she answered.

"They can really affect kids. They can make a kid believe in herself. They can help kids love math like I do," she said, her eyes growing larger and more teary with each sentence.

"Is that huge?"

"Yes.

Daphne had, in this case, attached a negative identity to a profession that would have really been a shame for her to overlook.

She ended up interviewing for several very good schools and then taking a job with an education industry company that would put her in touch with teachers and kids, but not necessarily in the role of teacher. Even though she saw her misguided assumption, I think it was very hard for her to really go for teaching whole-heartedly. I am sure it's not the last time she'll consider it, but for now, she'll build another professional identity she can live with.

GENDER IDENTITY

Not to worry, we are not talking about gender confusion here, but rather the changing roles of men and women in society and how they are making our world, our choices, and our decisions more complex. The advancements women have made in the workplace are huge and to be acknowledged. Until women make equal money dollar for dollar to men, there is still work to do. However, one aspect of these advancements that was per-haps unexpected by the women's movement is the confusion that it causes in the home between men and women who are a couple and in the world as competent and self-sufficient men and women bump up against one another.

Although we are decades away from the original, traditional roles of the woman being the caretaker of the family and home and the man being the financial provider, our wiring seems to be having trouble adjusting. We know on an intellectual level that it's OK for both men and women to share the home responsibil-ities and the onus of an income, but in many instances it is wreaking havoc on marriages and relationships. A lot of couples compete with each other or feel disappointed in the relationship if the financial onus changes. It is again about knowing the core of yourself as someone whose value is intrinsic in order to survive the chaos of these changes.

What is most important, however, is recognizing how gender expectations may make it difficult for you to make a transition. These changes need to be negotiated within a committed relationship or marriage and often need to be negotiated within oneself. If you don't think it's possible for you to succeed because of your sex or because of the track record for your sex based on what you want to accomplish, you are more likely to stop yourself from something that could make you happy. For a lot of women it means going for something they want in the workplace and for a lot of men that means being comfortable with a backseat or stay-at-home role.

As I mentioned earlier, according to the Bureau of Labor Statistics, one in three women outearns her spouse. Men whose identities are not wrapped up in their jobs are often taking on the role of stay-at-home parent to make the domestic picture work. How we are looking at these men and women has not yet gelled in our collective psyche. Others wonder what's wrong with the nonearning male spouse or make assumptions about the woman's character as a parent. On the other hand, we are also questioning the woman who steps off a high-level career track to spend more time with her children. Many of those women feel they are perceived as being on the "mommy track" and not interested in advancement, which is, for the most part, just not true. So, the point is that although we are going through the motions, our inner life has not really wrapped itself around the idea of transitioning out of conventional roles. We are not comfortable with it yet.

How it relates to us for the sake of an identity that hinders our ability to make a change of careers or lifestyle is to see that we have to be clear about which part of us is really "us" and which part of us is created by the expectations of our roles. As it stands, we trade wholeness for approval. We give away pieces of ourselves in order to color within the lines. If you are confused, that's OK. Many of us are. Future generations will have an easier time of this, but we'll have to muscle through it. The exercise later in this chapter will help.

MULTIPLE IDENTITIES

Wallace was a renaissance man (musician, painter, sports enthusiast) who came from a long line of family wealth. He was a businessman. He owned three companies and was a gifted scientist by training. He had three children and a wife and came to coaching to find a way to do all that he wanted to do well, without compromising anything. This was a tall order and not one that I suspected would take the form he had hoped, but we rolled up our sleeves and got to work.

There were so many pieces to the puzzle that made up Wallace's life that I knew he would have to come to terms with what needed to stay and what needed to go in order to make any sense of it all. This realization, of course, had to come from him and not me in order for him to understand that keeping all the balls in the air was not likely. What was at the crux of the discoveries he needed to make was exploring his identity. Wallace had never shed any of the layers of identity he had taken on over the years. What I mean by that is he let very little go as new interests, opportunities, and circumstances came his way. He was like a moving van that kept picking up belongings on a cross-country trek until it was bursting at the seams and causing its tires to shake under the pressure. He was a husband, a father, a trustee of the family estate, and the owner of three distinct businesses that required his presence, and he had many hobbies and interests, was on several charity boards, and had business and family obligations all over the globe.

Wallace claimed to love all of what he did and was not willing to give anything up, which basically meant that his success was in a holding pattern. There was no room to move or grow. It's like being on an overcrowded elevator and having the doors open up on a very large person who insists he will get on. There is nowhere to move to accommodate this change and that was where Wallace's life was. What finally began a shift was asking him to look at each piece he had taken on as a piece of an identity and challenging him to find out who he was today rather than being a product of every role and interest he had ever taken on.

This may sound strange at first, but if you think of it, each role in life comes with its own set of expectations. The father will provide, the businessman will be knowledgeable, the scientist will save the world, and the estate trustee must create more wealth and not take from the kitty without replacing what is taken. Each role Wallace held provided him with an identity. Who was he really? That is what we set out to find out.

Whittling a big life down to its core is sometimes like cutting through the bush with a machete; at other times it's like searching for a needle in a haystack. It can take broad strokes or gentle strokes, but there is always a new creation to be revealed. Usually, it is not really new. It appears as new because it has been buried for so long. Wallace revealed that at his core, he was a scientist and that is what he wanted to contribute. He quickly saw how everything he was involved with was a distraction from what he really felt he was meant to do.

Resigning from charity boards, selling one of his ventures, getting new partners involved, moving his main scientific business closer to his home, taking more time with his family, and delegating many family trust obligations were all ways for Wallace to get back to himself, his core, and his own happiness. In doing so he had to wrestle with his identity and how he saw himself in the world, but he did it and so can you.

Exercise: Check Your Identity at the Door

If you think you are having trouble getting ahead or reinventing your career because of a self-concept, follow the instructions here to help you gain clarity on your motivation and what may be blocking your success.

Record the roles you play in your life across the top of a page of paper. Employee, boss, husband/wife/partner, parent, community volunteer, son, sibling, and whatever other roles you fill. Now, in the space below each role write down your motivation for taking on that role at first and your motivation now for sticking with that role. By motivation I mean your reasons for being involved.

You'll need to be extremely honest with yourself. (That should not be new for you at this point in the book.) For example, yes, you may have become a boss because it meant more pay and status, but maybe part of your motivation for doing it was to show your nay-saying family that you could succeed above what they had expected from you.

The deeper internal motivations are important because they may show you some identity choices that you might want to change or that might help you understand how you got unhappy with something.

As you saw by doing the exercise above, there are often secondary motivations that help us form a false identity around our work or life roles that wreak havoc with our satisfaction level when they remain hidden from our consciousness. By bringing the true motivation to the surface, you are really free to choose who you want to be. It is very hard to shift gears when you cannot clearly identify what caused things to get off. What is often at the root of it is a false identity—an identity that you borrowed, took on, or forgot to shed, or that was thrust upon you when you weren't looking. This is the time to choose again.

Ease the identity crisis.

It's All in How You See It

▼

1. Realize that what keeps you stuck may be an identity issue.
2. Determine which external image or expectation got you stuck.
3. Get at your real motivation for taking on what you have.
4. Choose differently if it will set you free to make a change.

ELEVEN

Banking on a Miracle—
How to Chase Your Dreams,
yet Deal with What's Real

"I know this is it. If this works out, I've got it made."

NICHOLAS HAD HIS OWN SMALL BUT POWERFUL EXECUTIVE placement firm where he headed up a team of five employees. He came to work with me to make that business grow. In the meanwhile, he also fancied himself a venture capitalist and was busy raising money for a deal overseas that would capitalize on new free trade and capitalism in the Baltic. He was optimistic as he was approaching his fiftieth birthday, and he intended to celebrate big. He had an excessive way about him and a fierce drive to succeed that made me suspicious, but I did not have all the information yet.

Nicholas, as it turned out, had five homes in some of the hottest resort areas in the United States. He owned a Mercedes, lived in Manhattan, and had a country home nearby as well. He hadn't paid taxes in several years, and he had numerous other debts. He was even having trouble making payroll. Things had not gone so well in the last several years, but he didn't want a few debts to disrupt the life he had built for himself. He had worked hard to accumulate assets and was proud of his playboy image. He would not heed my warning that he was flirting with disaster, because he was courting some investors who he thought would not only get his overseas deal to fly, but would get him out of his own personal complications. He could not see that he was missing true success by denying the truth and grasping at straws, hoping to be saved by a miracle. He wanted me to support him as he layered more lies on these lies, refusing to clean up the mess he had created.

I said no, told him that when he was ready to deal with the real issue at hand I could help, and called off the coaching relationship just hours before I received a notice from my bank that his check to me had bounced. By the time I called him to straighten out our financial agreement, something had clicked with him. He was ready to play the game my way. I wasn't. "When you've been to Debtors Anonymous and have a plan for your financial recovery, we can resume," was how I left it with him.

Within four weeks, Nicholas had faxed me his plan, and we were back on. It was painful for him every step of the way, but in the next eighteen months, he sold all his vacation properties, paid most of his taxes with the profits and had a payment plan for the rest, sold his Mercedes and bought something more modest, and was feeling better than he had in a long time. He would not let go of the country home, but started renting it out to defray the expense. The overseas deal never did work out, but when he focused fully on his placement firm, the company was in the black. By the time we were wrapping up our work together, he had plans for another entrepreneurial venture, but he was not going to act on it until he had the financial reserve to do so. "I want to pay off the last of the credit cards and have some more money in the bank," he said. Ah, music to my ears.

Are you banking on a miracle to save you or your business? I hate to tell you this, but you are going to be waiting a long time. Living for a future that you anticipate, although there is no present indication that it is possible, is like jumping off a building because you believe you can fly. We have not been able to believe our way to fighting gravity and we haven't found a way to overcome personal financial ruin by waiting for the tooth fairy. Until you have the power of the U.S. government, you'll find it hard to maneuver in your world with a huge deficit. There are no miracles here; only responsibility and purposeful action will give you another shot at success.

I want to be sure that banking on a miracle is not confused with the Fish Tank Theory, which says you should shoot a bit beyond where you are now and grow into it. When you bank on a miracle, you're doing more than shooting a bit beyond where you are now. You are going beyond your means and taking unsupported risks. The Fish Tank Theory asks you to take the next graduated step even if you don't feel you are quite ready for it. You don't have far to fall if it doesn't work, although you will not fail often. If you go too far, maybe three or five or ten graduated steps beyond where you are, with no net to catch you, you are banking on a miracle and inviting a flop.

Nicholas never could articulate what finally made him stop his charade, but I think he realized his life could be a lot easier

if he just told the truth about it. Keeping up his rich playboy fa-
cade and living his life according to what other people would
think became too big a burden to bear. In the end, he found it
easier to start from scratch than to persist in trying to keep his
Titanic from sinking. Only when he was willing to take responsibility for cleaning up the mess and facing the truth did things
start to turn in his favor. As they say, "The truth shall set you
free." He stopped worrying about what other people would
think and began telling them the truth. If they knew the truth,
he would have nothing to hide and no fear of what they would
think. If your life is too dramatic for you, take a look at where
you aren't telling the truth. In a soap opera, two things move
the drama forward: someone tells a lie or someone withholds
the truth. If your life looks like a soap opera, with the exception
of a natural disaster or death, you can pretty much bet that a
variation or omission of truth is at the heart of it.

Getting at the Truth

What is the truth about your life and how you keep it afloat?
Does the truth hurt? What is it costing you to do it the way
you are doing it? Only when the cost gets too high will you
really do something about it. I am inviting you to do something about it before then. Save yourself a lot of trouble, and
admit that there is something wrong, so you can start putting
the pieces back together now. If you're not sure if this really
applies to you, you may not be reading all the signs that you
are headed for trouble. Are your knuckles white from holding
on for dear life? That could be a sign, but others might be
more subtle. For example:

Friends seem more distant.

You try to look good for all your friends and colleagues, but it's getting harder and harder.

You can't get anyone to lend you money anymore.

Bills are getting paid later and later.

You are fast to blame others and circumstances for your problems.

You are distracted and can't focus on work.

You're getting sloppy in your personal and business dealings.

You find yourself blabbing a lot about what you are going to do but not doing anything about it.

There will be signs in your work life too, whether you own your own business or navigate an organization:

Key employees start leaving.

The company is getting bigger and better but is not becoming more profitable.

You can't get loans from banks.

Debt is mounting fast.

Everything is at crisis proportions.

You can't seem to do anything right.

You'd rather be doing something else.

All these messages are telling you to pay more attention to the wholeness of your life and business. It's a call for action, but unless you're ready to hear the call, you are probably assuming things will get better. They will only get better if you make them better. It is crucial that you look for the source of the negative symptoms that are showing up in your life. Most people, if they are being responsive, automatically address the symptoms, but if you want to get back to health you need to address the source of each problem. Eliminate the source and the symptom won't return.

Eddie was a business owner I coached for a short time. He was starting a new business after his partnership in another business broke up. He hired me to get his new firm up to speed as fast as possible. He needed me to help him get organized, and his time management was terrible. He claimed that was why he and his business were such a mess. I knew this was just a symptom; I would find out more as I kept looking for the source of the chaos. By our second session, he started giving me honest answers to my questions. "What is *really* going on, Eddie?" It was more than I needed to hear. He was having an affair, he was drinking and carousing late into the night, and he had so much personal debt that he needed his business to make big money, and fast. As long as he needed a miracle, he wasn't going to get one.

If he were willing to take responsibility and clean up all the places where he was out of integrity, he might have a chance for turning his business and life around. He thought the solution was to get out there and sell more. That was sound reasoning, but he was the only salesperson (his staff was administrative or operational), he couldn't afford to hire anyone else, and there weren't enough hours in the day to make as many sales as he needed to turn a profit. Eddie's route to personal and business profitability was very clear and not out of his reach. Only his ego was in his way.

Eddie owned a multimillion-dollar home and had six luxury cars in the driveway. The cars were paid for, but the house was going to break him. When I requested that he sell the house, it was not the first time he had toyed with the idea. He had had it on the market before, but he took it off because he couldn't admit that he was not the same guy who had bought the house during better days. He also ignored my requests to sell the cars and reduce his staff. He knew he was digging his own grave, but he felt something would turn it all around and make it better. Every request I made of him to clean up his act went unheeded, so there was no point in my continuing to be his coach. I can only invest in clients who are ready to invest in themselves. I cannot be their winning ticket in the lottery they choose to play. I don't know what happened to Eddie, but he is a great example. There was nothing wrong with his business other than the fact that he didn't have enough capital because he needed to draw too big a salary. He thought his time management was the problem. Nope, just a symptom of a much bigger concern.

What are the sources you should be looking for? Here are some common causes that might hold some clues for you:

You assume the money will always be there.
You are living above your means.
You sweeten the truth (about anything).
You have weak personal and professional relationships.
You avoid handling a physical or emotional problem.
You let needs run amok (not getting them met).
You hold on to a past hurt or disappointment.
You are buried under myriad tasks, projects, or ideas that
     you never get to.

You must uncover the sources of problems in your business or organization. Look to what is at the bottom of the problem. It could be:

You assume the business will automatically grow.

Overhead is too high.

Productivity is down because of heavy paperwork (automation may be needed).

Staff is not properly trained or qualified.

Managers are ineffective.

You are not listening to your customers or the marketplace (they no longer want what you have).

You are draining the business profits that should go toward growth.

You and the company are crisis driven instead of solution oriented.

Christopher and I had been working together for a couple of months on expanding a new division of his accounting firm. It was a totally different business, and he was the partner in charge of it. It had been going for six months before I came along, and it had not brought in any revenue. He relied on a couple of people to do the prospecting and sales, and he supervised the whole operation. For the first two months he kept looking to me for ideas and strategies to increase sales. I gave them to him, but I kept saying that this was only a Band-Aid solution. The source of his problem was that the people he had on board did not know how to sell and had no expertise in this new area he had entered. Christopher disagreed: "No, no, no; I have to give them a chance."

He did give them a chance, but finally it came time to replace them. He was nervous about paying more money to someone more experienced, but I convinced him he could afford one person to replace the two he let go. Within one month, the new woman brought in more revenue than they had seen there in the previous eight months combined. Now he could afford another person of the same caliber. I think you get the picture. Don't put Band-Aids on the problem. Get to the source!

THE LOTTO MENTALITY— HOW TO TURN IT INTO A LIFE SAVER

The Lotto Mentality, thinking that some unforeseen windfall will make everything OK, is the mind-set that takes over when you make a life of banking on a miracle. It can be a blessing and a curse. In the context of this chapter, it has been working against you until this point. Your unwillingness to face the truth has kept you from taking action that would be best for you and your business. You've been waiting for a miracle, but there is a way to turn the Lotto Mentality into an asset. You can start to make it work for you.

Your ability to believe in miracles is a sign that you have tremendous faith in things turning out for the best. That is the blessing in all this. The problem is that this faith has no anchor. It's out there like a missile without a destination, floating around, hoping to bump into a target. Now, if this intense belief were rooted in responsibility, you could take an active role in helping that faith find a target, and get the results you were hoping for. You have a talent that you have turned against yourself, but a few adjustments will allow that talent to thrive. Action with faith might just invite that miracle. In my experience with clients it has never happened the other way around. I have never seen utter miracles happen because of pipe dreams, but I have seen the miraculous achievement of improbable goals that were supported by the right action.

I recently coached a journalist whose work has been featured in major periodicals and magazines all over the world. Her dream had always been to write a book about her very unusual, continent-hopping life. It was one of those things she hoped would drop out of the sky. She thought this would make her rich and save her from the unpredictable life of a freelance journalist. Bah humbug. Our first piece of business was to teach her to feel satisfied with her current situation so she no longer needed to be "saved" from it, and she could pursue a book deal from a more powerful position.

She raised her standards. She redesigned her portfolio to reflect a classy, solid representation of her and her work. In the past she had used her good reputation, but she did not present herself or her work in a way that reflected an appropriate level of professionalism. She also stopped taking work that was unsuitable for her income goals and more actively approached the publications she did want to work for. She landed some great assignments, and within seven weeks of our working together, she met an agent at a cocktail party who became very interested in her book idea. The agent asked to see a proposal and a sample chapter.

OK, you choose. Was it a coincidence, or did her miracle find her because it was anchored and had a target? Why would she get this opportunity now, after she had been hoping for at least a decade? It happened because she was getting her act together. She was taking decisive, purposeful action, taking great care of herself and her business, expecting the best, and asking for what she wanted. Her disappointment in her circumstances was gone. She turned her Lotto Mentality into something that could work for her, and her miracle found her. Desperation and need would have kept it far at bay. Instead, by taking her ability to dream and fueling it with action, she invited opportunity.

* * *

The physical world is an energy field. When you take action, you are sending electrical impulses into that energy field, teaching it what you want it to throw back at you. When you hope, you are actually hoarding those electrical impulses. They stay with you and don't enter the energy field. No wonder nothing comes back; you never sent the message out. Action is your message to the physical universe. It says you're serious about getting what you want. As long as there are no other obstacles to those impulses going out, the response you're looking for will come back.

You can argue this. What about those people who work diligently at something to no avail? If you are all action but have no faith, no ability to believe that the best will happen, that you somehow have to control everything if it is going to happen at all, you've blocked the good work those electrical impulses were trying to do. You need that rare balance of faith and action to make things work effortlessly. Sometimes, you're just not getting the message that it's time to pack it in. It never ceases to amaze me that we will keep doing the same thing over and over again when it is not working. Don't we get it? It's a message to try something else. It's like screaming louder and louder at a deaf person. She can't hear you. Try sign language or write it down. Just change tactics!

BASICS VS. NEEDS VS. DESIRES

If you clear up the mess you have allowed to permeate the present, you invite a great future. The simplicity of this idea dupes people into thinking it doesn't apply to them. Even the most successful people get seduced by this occasionally. There is a natural order to achieving what you want for your life and business that I haven't seen anyone bypass. You must attain the basics before you can meet your needs, and you must meet your needs before you can reach your desires. Basics vs. needs vs. desires. The differences between them can seem murky. The distinctions can collapse, and that is when people find themselves in over their heads. Actually, they are three very distinct concepts.

The *basics* comprise integrity in the architectural structure of your life. They take precedence in the hierarchy as the starting place from which it will be easier to reach other accomplishments. If the basics are in place, action toward your goal will be more sustainable and fluent. The basics consist of the essentials for living and for carrying out business: enough money to live, enough capital to carry the business, enough resources, enough people to support you, enough time to take care of yourself, and the ever-important telling the truth, keeping your word to yourself and everyone else. The basics are the bottom-line essentials. Do you have yours in place? Without them, the road to success can be very bumpy. People exaggerate their ability to operate without having the basics in place. Some succeed, but most get stopped and wonder why they can't have what they want. If you have the basics in place, they can serve as a springboard for the rest. To avoid stopping and starting, your life and your business have to be whole. You want to build the foundation in concrete, not sand. That means no major pieces should be missing. An investment in time to put the basics in place will pay off in both the short and long term.

Needs are the next step in the hierarchy. Those forces that drive you will seduce you into believing that you don't need the basics in place to succeed. Remember, needs will be met at any cost, so if you don't keep an eye on them and meet them in healthy ways, they can go out of control. If you have the basics in place, they will be much easier to meet.

Once you've done all the hard work, the reward is reaching your *desires,* on the other end of the spectrum. They are the things or conditions you want. They can be as big or as small as you can conceive. Making $20 million a year, getting the dream position in a company, having more than enough time to enjoy family and the pleasures of life—these are the things that motivate you to explore your capabilities.

Now here comes the tricky part: If any of your desires are tremendously emotionally charged, they are becoming needs. Maybe you would love to have the latest computer equipment for your office. That want intensifies until it becomes a need. You feel it has become impossible to do your job well without the nuances of the equipment you want. Now you need to have it to be satisfied; you feel you will be better off with it than without it. Being without it is a source of frustration. If you were to get back to basics, you might find that your current computer is fine. A couple of upgrades on some existing programs would do the trick, and everything would be back in order. You really didn't need all the bells and whistles of the new machine. Maybe the need that was driving you was your need to have the best, to be ahead of the pack, or to simply have fun with a new toy. It doesn't mean you can't have it, but if it's an expense you can't afford, you have knocked the basics out of place. Overspending would put you out of financial integrity; you would be knocking a block out of your foundation.

Your desires, as small or as farfetched as you care to imagine, should feel pretty light and carefree. Even if you want the seemingly impossible, thinking about it should feel great. If it is worrisome, if its realization is critical, or if you will feel diminished if it isn't accomplished, then we've uncovered a need. Desires are at the top of the hierarchy, and it is tougher to get those things to come to fruition if the other two parts of the hierarchy are not in place. When you are shooting straight for your desires without taking care of the other two steps, you are vulnerable to the Lotto Mentality.

Matt came to work with me to get his career on track. When he followed the steps in the hierarchy, his progress accelerated and became consistent. He was just finalizing his divorce when we started working together. There were no kids and there was no money, so he was relatively unscathed, but trying to get his own life back on track. He had been a freelance production assistant on movie sets and commercials, and he aspired to move up the ladder to line producer someday. In the meanwhile, he had become accustomed to living hand to mouth, borrowing against his credit card to live. His debt became deeper every time he was between jobs. He was heavily in debt, and he did not have the basics in place. Our first step was to restore his financial integrity. He started to moonlight at odd jobs. He sold some of his belongings and moved into a much cheaper apartment with a roommate to further defray costs. An opportunity came along for an out-of-town job that would become the perfect vehicle to get rid of the rest of his debt. All his expenses would be taken care of on the job, so he subleased his half of the apartment in order to make the job pure profit.

Matt and I resumed our work together when he returned. He was completely debt-free and had managed to save some money. The basics were in place, and he could start taking care of his needs. He came back determined to send out résumés and do a lot of networking to get to the next level in his career. Within a couple of months, a director with whom he had worked before approached him about starting a production company; Matt would be the executive producer. Being an executive producer, especially in his own company, was even beyond his desires, but with money in the bank, he felt he could afford the challenge and the risk. He did need to borrow seed money, which he got from relatives and friends. He was determined not to allow his life to spin out of control again. As it turned out, within six months, he had paid everyone back, and he has been at the helm of a highly profitable, million-dollar-a-year business ever since.

All these scenarios illustrate what is possible when you take responsibility for the circumstances of your business and your life. Once these clients told the truth, they stopped feeling like victims and started taking drastic measures to improve their situations. If you are in a similar position, you need to simplify your business and your life. It's time to set yourself up to win by simplifying the game. It's time to get back at the helm of your life and stop being at the mercy of what is coming at you. Once you let go of worrying about what other people think and shed your own nonsense about being a failure, you'll find taking charge rewarding. It will also be a huge relief to stop living the lies and the guilt. Ready to simplify? Oh, wait. I can still hear you balking. You think that you can't make these kinds of radical changes if there is family to consider. Don't worry about them; get them involved. Everyone needs to be in on the simplification process, family and employees alike. You'll need all the support you can get to turn around your business and your life. We'll start with your business (or career).

1) **Reevaluate what works and what doesn't.** Stop blaming, and be ruthless in telling the truth about what is right or wrong with your business. Remember to look for the source of the problem instead of just patching holes. This is your opportunity to ask yourself why you are in this business anyway, and to decide if it is still worth going for it. Are you in it to make money? To enjoy the chase? To look good? To fulfill an obligation to carry on a family enterprise? Get back in touch with what matters to you, so you can commit to making this business work.

2) **Give it all you've got, reinvent it, or get rid of it.** To keep this business, you'll need to radically cut expenses and bring up your profitability by 100 percent. Figure out which people, resources, and systems you'll need to double your sales. To do this you may need to reinvent all or part of the business. Take radical action to adjust your profit centers so they are extremely profitable and easy. You may develop new products and services, so there is more to sell. Finally, if you're going to let it go, is it salable? If you have to get it in shape to sell it, maybe it's worth keeping. Think hard, and commit to whichever path you choose wholeheartedly. If you can't commit 100 percent, it is a pretty sure bet that it's time to let it go.

3) **Secure your support system.** Don't keep the people around you in the dark. You can't turn this ship around if you don't tell the crew what's going on. Get cooperation from everyone. You'll need their energy to go full swing into simplifying and turning the business around. Your personal needs must be met, and you can't afford any naysayers. Get family, friends, and staff to rally behind you.

4) Get back integrity and raise your standards. No cheating. There is no easy way out. Decide what you stand for and operate your business that way. Take the high road; don't be tempted to save yourself or the business by taking any shortcuts. Raise the stakes. Get all work up to snuff. Employees who aren't pulling their weight must go. Go back to your customers, and take care of them as you never have before. Listen to them for clues that could help you serve them better.

5) Build a reserve. Start putting money in the bank even before you can afford to do so. Reward employees who save the company money. Get on a conservative plan that will allow you maximum profits and savings. Build up a reserve before you allow any more growth in the company. Buckle down and get solvent!

When you need less cash from the business, you will ease the tension that may be what was causing business problems in the first place. The steps to simplifying your business can then be reflected in simplifying your life.

1) Know where the money goes. Show me the money. Show me where it goes. You probably don't really know; you're not alone. Most people are better at this in their businesses than they are in their lives. Track every dime you spend for a month. Have everyone else in your household do the same. This is not fun; it's shocking. It won't be painful for long, though. One month of recording should be enough to give you a picture of how much you spend in incidentals. You will need this information for the following steps.

2) Make a budget. Using the information you gathered, make a budget that reduces your expenses by 25 to 40 percent. Impossible, you say? I don't care. Do it anyway. You need to see instant profitability. This is how you will get that. Downsize to a smaller home, make it on one car, fire the housekeeper. Whatever you have to do to reduce those expenses must be done. No more hoping it will get better. It won't until you get things back on track. Once you've designed the budget, share it with your family and support system, and stick to it. Stop balking, and just do it.

3) Bring in additional income. You're going to have to hustle and move fast. Sell expensive items you can part with, moonlight, rent out a room in your house, turn a hobby into a moneymaker. Get creative; come up with ways to bring in extra money.

4) Save while you pay down debt. Take 10 percent of everything you bring in during this simplification process and put it in an account you will not touch. Use the rest of your profit to pay off debt. It is just as important for you to see a reserve building as it is to see the debt reducing. When you have finished paying the debt, do not increase your spending. Put what you were putting toward debt into savings. When you can keep three to six months' expenses as a cushion with no effort, only then will you be ready to start spending again.

Blaire worked with me for three to six months, three years in a row. She was used to living on the edge, and she liked it. She believed that when she needed money it would always be there. She had the faith of the Lotto Mentality, and although it wasn't working totally against her, it wasn't working for her either. The first two times we worked together, we were successful in improving her business and strengthening her personal and business relationships, but we never had an impact on her money life. She would readily admit to overspending, but she didn't see anything wrong with carrying some credit card debt, regardless of the interest rates. She still didn't see any reason to save money, because she had always found it when she needed it, even if it was with interest.

The last time we worked together, however, her situation had changed. She was now a single mother, and this reality sobered her; she was ready to give financial integrity another try. She finally recognized that getting by was just not good enough anymore. Having more than enough money was now what she expected of herself. And she did it! She started by putting her child support checks in an untouchable account. If she stopped her compulsive shopping, she could make it on what she made and use the support checks to invest in her daughter's education. Saving started to feel better than shopping. She kept looking for more ways to save. She finally could hear and take action on what we had been talking about for years. She started to save 10 percent of everything she made as well as chipping away at her debt. She paid herself first; before, there had never been anything left to save. When she paid herself first, she forced herself to make it on what was left. She now claims she's addicted to saving. I'd rather she were not addicted to anything, but at least it's more positive.

Evan was a stockbroker in his early forties when he suffered a devastating financial loss in the rocky stock market of the late 1980s. He had been living the adrenaline-high life, and when he lost so much, he decided to pack it in. He had been a high-roller type of risk taker and had never really prepared for a blow like this. He wasn't sure what he would do next, but he figured he could find a way to parlay his talents into some form of consulting. He was amazed to be so wealthy in one moment and so much in the red in the next. Nonetheless, he licked his wounds and decided to put the pieces back together. He took out all the stops. He moved his wife and young son from their large luxury apartment (which he rented out at a profit) to a small two-bedroom apartment in a less ritzy part of town. He sold his BMW and got rid of all the luxury items that would cash in at a good price. Between what he sold and some savings, he had enough money to keep his family going for a while. His newfound freedom from the trappings of a better life actually felt good. He took a couple of months to recover from the years of the high life, and then he put his mind to setting himself up as a private financial planner and advisor. Within eighteen months, he had built his clientele and was bringing in enough income to start upgrading his lifestyle again. This time, he had different criteria. He always had an ample reserve, and he no longer believed in living beyond his means and pretending that this could never backfire. He had found a new way to enjoy his success.

Take responsibility and you'll invite a miracle.

Wait for a miracle and it will never come.

Stop Wishing, and Start Turning Around Your Life and Business

▼

1. Tell the truth to yourself and to everyone else.
2. Get to the source of every symptom.

3. Get plenty of support.
4. Simplify! Downsize!
5. Become profitable immediately (cut expenses, liquidate, moonlight, add products or services).
6. Restore integrity.
7. Put money in the bank.
8. Congratulations; you saved yourself!

TWELVE

▼

The Elusive Gift— Self-Discipline

"I know this. The question is, why don't I do it?"

I HEAR THIS ON MANY A COACHING CALL. YOU KNOW WHAT TO DO; you just don't do it. You need to hear it over and over to get it into your psyche. The point of this book, and the whole reason that people hire a coach, is: DO it, don't just know it. Intellectualizing something gets you nowhere; getting it into your muscle memory will. Both your brain and your muscles have a memory. That's why you can be a klutz at a new sport one day and wake up the next morning much improved. It gets into your muscle memory, and you perform better. This is true of all the information you are taking in here. It must get into your muscles to be effective. Reading it or hearing it is not enough; you will have to practice so it can become an integrated part of who you are.

Self-discipline is elusive for a lot of people. They are envious of those who can do tough things that will get them what they want and where they want to go. For most there is a constant inconsistency between being who they want to be and doing what they have to do to be that person. Why is it so hard? There are three major factors at work here. The first is *adrenaline* (see chapter 3). It keeps you going so fast and flying so high that you're on autopilot, and you don't have the presence of mind to be disciplined about many of the things that matter to you. The second is *self-worth*, knowing at the deepest level that you are worth doing these great things for yourself. Of course you're worth it, so what's the struggle about? The third factor is *structure*. You make demands of yourself but then don't put aside the time or create the proper support to make it happen. These three problems cause you to stop and start, thwarting your best intentions. You may go through three stages of growth in developing discipline to help you conquer this once and for all. Before you get there, however, there are a few things to keep in mind.

The way to develop discipline is to put yourself first. If you let life and circumstances knock you off your block, you're putting yourself at the mercy of someone (or something) else. Discipline comes from valuing who you say you want to be more than anything else, holding true to your vision for you and not cheating yourself at every turn. It's deciphering the real you from the knee-jerk-reaction you. You must become conscious of when the impostor who wants to betray your best intentions is fighting for attention, and you must not give in.

You'll have to develop an ability to give to yourself freely. You'll have to increase your ability to have. If you can't discipline yourself to save money, maybe you don't really think you're worth the effort. If you can't make it to the gym because you don't have time, you're saying you're not worth the time. If you can't pull yourself away from the TV to do something productive, you're declaring you're not worth it. Sounds harsh, but I'm sure you can find the truth in it. So, what to do? Put yourself first. Take extremely good care of you. Expand your ability to give more to yourself. This has a cumulative effect; once you start seeing the difference in how you feel, and give yourself the thing that will reflect who you want to be, you won't stop doing it and you'll move on to the next thing you want to discipline yourself to include.

With that in mind, let's take a look at the three stages you may go through in developing discipline. You may have completed some of these stages already in your current strides toward accomplishment, so adopt the stage that describes what you are ready for and graduate to the next one from there. Where you are in your personal development will determine which will work for you now. You won't need me to help you decide. You'll know when you try each one on for size. If it appeals to you, do it.

THE FIRST STAGE—STRUCTURE

You beat yourself up because you didn't do something, but you are swatting at a symptom. The real problem is that you never created a structure within which it could get done. When you build something, you start with a framework, a structure that supports the rest of the creation. To write this book, I started with an outline. To build a house, you put up the frame first. Before we build a business, we strategize and write up a plan. It is surprising that most people do not have a framework to support their daily lives. They need a structure to support the person who is going to accomplish the goals.

It's the little things that make a difference in this instance, the things that get pushed aside because you think you don't have enough time. Yet they are exactly the things that would keep you at peak performance. I know you know exactly what I mean: exercising, eating well, acknowledging the important people in your life every day, the calls that would make the difference, doing the professional reading you've been meaning to do. It will mean putting these things first and watching everything else fall in place. Your car needs regular maintenance. If you get too busy to bring it in for maintenance, you'll find yourself taking it in later on for something bigger and more expensive. Your regular maintenance schedule is the structure that supports the health of the car. The same goes for you. Graduate from seeing yourself as a machine and, instead, see yourself as a finely tuned instrument that needs great care to perform well. That great care will be supported by the structure you create for it.

This balance is the single greatest challenge for executives and business owners. Strong support, good business systems, and a solid personal framework will all contribute to striking the balance that frees you from the grips of finite time and helps you to feel disciplined. We are going to design a personal framework that will serve as an indelible guidepost around which the rest of the day's activities can fall into place. It's like putting up the frame to a house. Once it's up, you can make the house look any way you want it to, but it has to be there. We want to put this kind of infrastructure into your life, so no matter what you weather, your structure will still stand, and it will help you develop discipline.

Your Daily Framework

List the specific, daily actions that would support what you are up to. Choose as many as you can reasonably apply to your day. Five to ten is a good start. Your list should reflect both business and personal actions that would support your well-being. Many people make the mistake of creating a wish list. For example, they will write down: do my work on a timely basis, spend more time with family, exercise more. These will not work because they are not specific. Our purpose is to create a framework around which everything else will fall into place, so the daily actions that you create for yourself have to be in action form. When they are specific, they are measurable, and you'll be more likely to do them. They will sound more like this: make the toughest call of the day first, block out thirty minutes a day for correspondence, check e-mail only twice a day to avoid distractions.

Create the framework with actions that will support the goals you have for your life and career. If you are working on increasing sales, you may have a daily plan about how many calls a day you will make. If you are creating visibility for yourself in a company, your framework might include daily contact with key people. If you're starting a business, you may include telling five people a day what you are working on. The business and work habits should be interspersed with your habits of well-being to develop discipline on both sides.

More samples:

Have fifteen minutes of silence a day.

Eat lunch away from my desk.

Make five business development calls a day.

Clear my desk at the end of the day.

Connect with managers daily via e-mail.

Drink eight glasses of water a day.

Connect with my spouse daily.

Read the *Wall Street Journal.*

Take twenty minutes every morning for planning.

| Return calls from 2 to 4 o'clock daily. | Leave by 6:30 P.M. every day. Walk thirty minutes a day. |

Ross struggled terribly with making time in his life to be attentive to his family. He allowed himself to be consumed by work because he was trying to get a new business off the ground. He was wracked with guilt, and until he started working with me, he could not get on top of things well enough to bring a balance back to his life. We jumped right in and created a structure for his day that allowed him to get home to his family at a reasonable hour. He took the first hour to do all his phone calls so that he caught people at their desks or knew he could expect a call from them sometime during his day. He spent the last thirty minutes of his day cleaning his desk and making a to-do list for the following day. In between, he integrated a daily call home and daily contact with the people he delegated to, and he blocked out time to do his work when he would not be interrupted. As a result of his daily framework (which he looked at daily, checking off each task as he did it), he created a routine that supported all his goals, including getting home early. He had stopped allowing his day to snowball on him. His guilt was gone, his family was happy, he was happy, and business took off. He allowed himself to have the time with his family, and business never suffered. He developed the discipline to finish on time every day by honoring his framework and honoring his priority as a family man.

Now What?

Once you have your list, the hard part is integrating it. Some people dive right in and do everything on the list right away. Others concentrate on two until they become habits and then add two more until those are habits, and so on. You decide, but get going. These habits are especially important for sole proprietors or those who are completely self-generating, because this list will need to become your default mechanism. If there is a day when you hit a wall, forgive yourself and just focus on your framework actions. Get the framework back in place, and before long, the rest will fall into place.

Peter was the chief financial officer of a $10 million firm who came to me to help him with a plan to find a new job. In the meantime, I also coached him on how to pay attention to what was going on for him in the present, in order to make life more bearable until the new opportunity came along. His frustration was obvious, and the stress was straining his relationships at home.

He complained about being treated unfairly by his bosses and about the lack of consideration that pervaded his office environment. He was constantly subjected to interruptions and could barely hear himself think.

He worked with me for ninety days, he learned some new management skills, and the action he took eventually landed him a great job, but the biggest impact came from the smallest change. In helping him create his framework, I requested that he lunch outside the office every day. It seemed like a simple request, but it had a tremendous impact. Going out for lunch allowed him to think more clearly at work, to be more efficient with his time, and to have more patience with his staff. It forced him to have a meal that he usually skipped. Most important, the bickering and mood swings, which were affecting his relationship with his wife and the quality of time he spent with his young son, stopped. That one bit of structure had a powerful ripple effect.

Peter was falling into the trap of ignoring his own maintenance in order to keep up with the demands of the job. He had lost all discipline by being at the mercy of circumstances. He was not valuing himself enough to put himself first. As he came to understand this, he saw that nothing was going to change in his environment until he himself changed. He had let his day become one big overwhelming wave. He lacked a structure that could define his day and give him a sense of accomplishment. After he put his maintenance first, he had the energy to turn his work situation into something he could live with instead of something that was eroding him. Once his work situation was stabilized, he was a more attractive job candidate and he had more time and energy to devote to his job search and to the other things that mattered to him. The signals that caused his environment to change had to come from him. It would never have worked the other way around. His daily framework fostered the discipline he needed to keep his whole life in control.

THE SECOND STAGE—DO LESS, BE MORE

So far, you have been *doing* a lot to develop your gift for discipline. It is crucial that you have the structure and create the time and space to do the things for which you need more discipline. However, as Thomas Leonard proposes, the next frontier to this odyssey of self-discipline is the question "Who do I want to *be*?" "What do I want to do?" is important too, but the Who has to come first to make it all work. Even our best intentions are thwarted when we stick only to what we want to do to achieve a specific result. To take the higher road for ourselves, we must ultimately attach its value to who we want to be. I often ask clients, "Now that we have all the action steps planned out to reach your goal, who are you going to have to be to attain it?" Oh, yes, it's usually met with an appropriate pause. That's because you're not used to thinking that way.

The struggle with weight loss can illustrate what I mean. Almost everyone I've worked with—no matter how powerful, wealthy, or established, and no matter how business oriented our work is—wants to be in better physical condition, one of the toughest things our culture has tried to be disciplined about. Usually you make up a strict list of Whats—things to do to be disciplined about getting in shape: no eating after 8 P.M., exercise four times a week, fruit and vegetables daily, no fats, no sugar, and so on. You might only stick to that list while your enthusiasm for it lasts. Then you run out of steam. You created a structure for accomplishing the goal, and that's good. What's missing is attention to who you have to be to be physically fit. If you frame it in terms of who you have to be to attain this goal, you will increase your chances of sticking to it.

You might say, "To reach this goal, I have to be someone who honors her body, someone who only hangs out with healthy people, someone who moves her body in a healthy way every day, someone who puts only nourishing foods in her body." The What list will lose its effectiveness when you start to feel deprived. In contrast, the Who list challenges you to go beyond your comfort zone. It stretches you; it asks you to become more. We are much less threatened and much more inspired by the prospect of being more. Being strict, being disciplined, loses its appeal. These are progressive steps; we need those linear actions to get us going, but the Who level will sustain us in reaching our goal.

Getting to Where You Want to Be

Go back to your daily framework and add a second list of items that reflect who you have to be to achieve your goals. If there is a linear action that you will need to support that, change your daily framework to include it.

I was in a meeting with a young editor at a publishing house. She was kicking herself for having missed an opportunity that she was convinced could have been a career maker for her. She longed to be like the senior editor who supervised her. She already knew what she needed to do, and there was no use in rehashing that. Instead, I asked her who she had to be now to become that senior editor. She paused and then suddenly seemed to break free of the beating she had been giving herself. Her eyes lit up, and she said, "I have to be someone who trusts her instincts enough to act on them." It was an "ah-ha." She knew that she should have acted faster when she discovered the opportunity, but this was forgotten when she realized that what really had to change was not her speed, but her ability to trust her instincts. If she had trusted herself, she would have acted on the opportunity sooner. Now she did not have to wait for another situation to *do* things differently; she could start *being* different right away.

THE THIRD STAGE—ACCEPTANCE

Structure and becoming who you want to be will work most of the time, but when they don't, you'll have no choice but to enter the third stage: acceptance. There are some things that you just may never be disciplined about. There is nothing wrong with that. You'll either come up with some other creative way to get the same result, or you'll give up the result altogether. This is not a cop-out; it's just a reflection of the contrast between internals and externals. If you can't get yourself to do something no matter how hard you try, it could very well be you didn't really want it in the first place. It was something you thought you *should* do. It may also be that you do want it, but you tried to do it in a way that was not organic to you.

For example, although I successfully ask many of my clients to make a certain number of prospecting calls a day as part of the discipline of growing their sales, this strategy never worked for Stacy. She tried to make herself do it, to the point of exasperation. When she told me of her struggle, we realized that those conversations were not using the best of what she had to offer. We looked at the result she was disciplining herself to achieve. Her business was new, and she wanted to gain more clients. She wasn't good at calling, but she was good at public speaking. The solution was clear: Stacy spoke everywhere she could until audience members turned into prospects. She accepted that she would never be good at making those calls, so she switched to something she could do well and got the same result, if not a better one.

What to Do with Your Shoulds

What part of your struggle to be disciplined needs rethinking? Ask yourself what you are trying to achieve, and focus on the strengths you can use to achieve it. Do it your way. Now, what about those things that you just don't get around to? Where does acceptance come in there? You know you *should* do your professional reading (the pile gathers more dust every day), you know you *should* exercise (the NordicTrack has become a coat-rack), you know you *should* put more away toward retirement (the prospectus makes a nice coaster). If creating your daily framework didn't work, and getting at the Who doesn't appeal to you, just give up. Accept that you won't get to it, and find another solution. Hire a trainer, pay someone to spoon-feed you the action you need to take, or find someone to share the burden with you. There are some things you want that you are just not good at and will never be able to motivate yourself to do. Don't feel bad about it. Find another way, or decide you can live without it. Trust yourself to find out what is really worth being disciplined about.

This brings me to the final frontier in developing discipline: trust. Trust yourself to do what really matters to you. When you give yourself that much credit, you don't have to be the whip master to foster discipline in yourself. Use structure and who you want to be as tools to guide you and train you. Eventually you'll break through. Discipline will be in your muscle memory, and you won't think about it anymore.

Physical fitness again is an easy, universal example. If you create a structure for a fitness routine and make the changes to who you want to be in adopting a healthy lifestyle, eventually you will experience such a great benefit that you won't need to be disciplined about it. At this point you wouldn't dream of giving it up. You've made the breakthrough to trust.

Blaire failed year after year at disciplining herself to save money until she internalized it and made it her goal, rather than what she should do. When getting by was no longer good enough, she was ready to do something about it. Then and only then could she discipline herself. She found the structure in which to do it, saw herself in a new light once the structure made it possible, and eventually she was able to trust that she would not lose ground.

Discipline is a kinder friend when you use it to support who you want to become. Stop using it to beat yourself up. When discipline is a punishment, it will have the opposite effect of the one you desire. Once you know who you want to be, what you have to do will become undeniably clear. Discipline will no longer be the elusive gift.

Be true to who you want to be, and discipline will follow.

Develop Self-Discipline

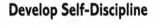

1. Make sure you're off adrenaline.
2. Adjust your mind-set; know you deserve the result you want.
3. Make yourself your number one priority.
4. Create your daily framework (a structure to achieve discipline).
5. Get at who you want to be, not just what you want to do.
6. Accept that you may need to find creative solutions to help you.
7. Enjoy knowing you can count on yourself. You've got discipline!

THIRTEEN

▼

Relationships—A Defining Factor in Taking Yourself to the Top

"Why do some people have an easier time becoming successful? Is it really all who you know?"

YOU WON'T GET TO THE TOP OF THE GAME OF LIFE WITHOUT other people. Operating in a vacuum won't get you there; understanding how relationships fit into the puzzle will. Relationships are a key factor in your success, not because of what other people can do for you, but rather because of who you can become by being in their presence. I don't mean that people with the right amount of power or status will help you become who you want to become (although that can help). I am saying that relationships exist to help you get a handle on who you are and who you want to become. You'll want to learn how to choose those that elevate you to the top.

Relationships are the vehicle by which your success will come to you. They are like the cilia that move a cell along its journey, supporting it, protecting it, and keeping it flexible while moving it along its path. Relationships will help you be your best if you choose them well. You know this is true. You know that no one is an island, and yet you don't pay enough attention to who accompanies you off that island and ultimately on your journey to the top.

HOW TO CHOOSE

When you start becoming conscious about your human connections, both professional and personal, when you raise your awareness about who you spend time with and whether or not they elicit your best, you run the risk of losing a couple of long-standing fixtures in your life. Some people have been in your life for a very long time just because you share a history or you feel a sense of loyalty to them, although they stopped contributing positively to your life a while ago. You risk losing them, but I know it is well worth it. To get to the top of your game, you will have to become very selfish. That includes rubbing obligation out of your repertoire and only forming and keeping relationships out of choice. *Choose* to have certain people in your life; *choose* to let others go.

There are essentially three types of relationships: those that will sink you, those that will float you, and those that will rocket you. What makes them different is the amount of energy they take from or give to you. Let's take a look at each one so you can recognize them when you are in them and focus your relationship-building efforts where they will count.

The energy-draining relationship—This is a lead weight dragging you down, holding you back, or sinking you altogether. Your energy is being siphoned, and yet you may not be aware of it. There could be signs of a co-dependency if your well-being is wrapped up in this person's well-being, or vice versa. The other person has to be OK for you to be OK. In its less dramatic form, this relationship requires a great deal of effort to work.

The energy-dependent relationship—This relationship is more like a flotation device. It's pleasant and it's equal in a tit-for-tat sort of way. Each person takes turns being dependent on the other, and it all works pretty well. The balance is not necessarily bad, but it is not extraordinary.

The energy-exchange relationship—This relationship is the rocket, but I'm not talking about the fireworks that are clichés for romantic relationships. I mean a business or personal relationship in which there is such a powerful exchange that the relationship becomes a conduit for creativity. The two people are so equal that when they get together, neither is stealing energy from the other, so there is enough energy to create with. These are the people with whom you tap into your best ideas, or invent something, or feel inspired by, or get in touch with the better parts of yourself. In other words, they bring out your best.

I am by no means suggesting that you dump people in your life because they go through a rough time and need more support from you. Any one relationship can go through these three levels at a given time. Just the same, look at the relationships in your life as these three types to determine who is great for you. Great people are not necessarily great *for* you, so be careful to make that distinction in choosing who you keep in your life. Does that sound harsh? Well, it's up to you. Why would you purposely keep people in your life who hold you back? If you don't think you have a choice, you are mistaken; there is always a way. If you choose to keep these people in your life, that is your prerogative; however, ask yourself why and set boundaries to what kind of time you spend with them.

"What about family? You don't have any choice about your family." Not true. You can redefine those relationships although they are steeped in tradition and, sometimes, bad habits. Ask them for what you need. Tell them what support looks like for you. Teach them how to be with you. Does that sound abnormal or unnatural? It's definitely uncommon, but it is the most natural thing in the world to right a relationship you have let be wrong for so long. A client of mine had been putting up with his brother's insensitive comments for years. They had had a history of ribbing each other and being verbally abusive as a way of showing support and affection. The brother who was receiving the coaching had outgrown this, and he began to avoid his brother. Once he understood that he could change the situation, he had a whole new approach the next time he saw his brother. He finally said, "You know, your support means a lot to me, but my definition of support has changed. I want to hear positive statements and praise instead of horsing around. Maybe I've gone serious on you, but that's what I need." It was hardly an issue. The direction and tone of the request changed their relationship instantly, and they were happy to be back together.

HOW TO FIND AND BUILD
RELATIONSHIPS THAT WILL ROCKET YOU TO THE TOP

By now, I'm counting on you being able to recognize and be honest about which relationships fuel you and which drain you. To create your way to the top, you can't afford any rust on your rocketship. You'll need to assemble a strong personal and professional community to support you. Most of the major changes you've been asked to make in this book included getting the right support to do so. That is why the right relationships are so important. They will afford you the luxury of making changes easily as well as helping you get your needs met. You'll feel like you have more than you need in terms of friendship, love, support, and opportunities.

Your Inside Ten

As part of your personal community, you'll want to grow a circle around you of ten people you can count on. They are on the inside of your life, and they can include family, friends, and people with whom you have close ties in your professional world. They are on the inside because they bring out your best. They are your buffer and cushion from negative influences. They are generous with you, and you with them. They can afford for you to succeed, and they don't feel threatened. They would never talk behind your back, and they always have your best interests at heart. It is a joy for you to be around them, and they feel the same way about you. If it is easy to be with them, they are eligible to be in your circle. Does this sound like a fantasy? It's not. You invite people into your life who don't need to fill a void in their lives with your friendship. They'd be fine without you and you without them, so you are in the relationship because it enhances both your lives.

Beth worked with me over the course of a year to improve her business skills in order to grow her interior design business. Building both personal and business relationships became part of our work together. When she tried to write down who would be in her inside ten, Beth was stumped. She realized that although she had many people in her life, her relationships didn't have the quality that would take her to the next level of satisfaction and support.

She was upset to recognize that most of the people in her life needed her for something, and that she was never really free to just enjoy herself with people. She became determined to change that. She directed some of the people who were already in her life to get away from needing her all the time and to use their friendship to enhance each other's life. They shared new information about each other and attended events that were of common interest. During some of those activities, they met other people who, over time, became part of Beth's inside circle. Of course, she and these people helped each other when they had problems, but drama was not the centerpiece of their relationships. Also, Beth's business grew 30 percent during the year that she formed her relationships differently. Much of her new business came from her inside ten and also from her improved business network.

Your Frontline Twenty

Are you keeping in touch with everyone you know professionally? If you're not, don't worry about it. It would be smarter to keep in touch with a targeted list of people that are truly your advocates, the people who tell the world how great you are without any prompting from you. These are the people who are in your fan club and go crazy in a room if your name comes up. These are the people who bring in business or opportunities for you simply because they believe in you wholeheartedly and share that fact freely. You want to build that quality of network up to at least twenty people. It can be larger, but it will need to be manageable. You will need to find a way to stay in touch with these people regularly, whether it's by phone, fax, or get-togethers, or if appropriate, through a newsletter about your business.

The theory behind the frontline twenty is that if you choose well, the twenty people you have chosen should multiply into many more. They are your front line out there, doing some of the work for you. These twenty people have many more people behind each of them that they know and can talk to about you. They may be the same centers of influence as the ones we discussed earlier. They will be sending along people like them who should be as great a match for you as the original frontline twenty members were. Best of all, this takes much less effort than chasing less qualified prospects. They come to you, instead of your having to run around and find them.

How do you get people to be in your fan club and qualify for your frontline twenty? It takes nurturing, attention, and putting yourself out there. Being shy will not be noble in this case. You'll need to be out there networking at industry events, company events, professional organizations, conferences, breakfast meetings, and any other legal way you can see and be seen. Once you have developed the beginning of your frontline twenty, it gets easier. The contacts begin to build on each other, and you graduate from getting in front of a lot of strangers to smaller, more intimate meetings where you really get a chance to get to know people. The hardest part is starting, and then it becomes effortless.

The quality of relationship you have with these people will make all the difference. Schmoozing is out. A genuine exchange of information on business trends and leads will be a helpful and solid way to begin building your network of professionals. The more people you know in different industries, the easier your time will be as well. When you become a walking Rolodex for anyone you meet that might need a service or product other than yours, you have served them in a way that makes a great opening for a business relationship. Another way to develop fans is to give them a chance to see you at work. If you do any kind of public presentation or demonstration, invite your would-be fans. The more they see of you on the job, the more they can tell about you. You may also volunteer in your community or in a professional organization. It's a great way to get more time with people and to have them witness you at your best.

Ron was a salesman who used to knock himself out trying to keep in touch with almost everyone he had been in contact with in the last year. When he switched over to building a frontline twenty list, he quickly saw who was really potential business for him and who wasn't. He put the people on his list who had been happy with his product and would be willing to talk about it. Over time, Ron found himself with a lot of time on his hands because he had taught his fans how to talk about him, and they were practically selling his product for him! As he nurtured his network, his business grew. He enjoyed talking to people anyway, so tending to his frontline twenty became his favorite activity. He got to give up doing his most unfavorite activity: cold calling.

SERVICE

The quality of relationship that will rocket you to the top depends equally on what you put into it and what you get out of it. If you are of service to other people personally and professionally, you will attract the people capable of a higher level of relationship to you. Nonetheless, it's a fine line between serving the people around you and getting caught up in doing for others at a cost to yourself. You will need to be aware of this, as you transform how you develop and keep relationships in your life. Use your internal barometer, your gut, to tell you when you are crossing the line into giving away the store at your own expense. To be a great friend, spouse, parent, or business associate, you must be generous of spirit but still selfish enough to keep yourself whole. If you feel resentful, compulsive, or drained, you know you have gone too far.

Being of service can mean actually doing something for someone else, or just giving generously your time, attention, or praise. This can feel somewhat forced at first if you are not used to it, but after a while it becomes a way of life. You won't know until you do it, but it can be very rewarding. However, you'll only be able to be this generous and not hurt yourself if you've already taken good care of yourself. If you're serving others before you've fully taken care of your own needs, or you're doing it to get something in return, you will be headed for a messy disaster.

Sarah, the executive recruiter, found it fun to give extra time to job candidates, even those she could not place right away. She had a talent for making people feel special, and although she did so with no strings attached, it often came back to her in the form of successful referrals or new clients. On the other hand, Louise, another recruiter, was spending countless hours on the phone being very helpful, but resenting every moment of it. The time she spent was time away from prospecting and placing candidates. She could not afford the freedom to give this level of service until the other parts of her business were working without her and she was not robbing herself to give to somebody else.

Here are some ways to be of service to people:

1) Tell them how great they are and why.
2) Give them more than they expect.
3) Contribute ideas to their businesses.
4) Give them qualified business leads, even when they don't ask for them.
5) Give money or volunteer time to a charity someone else supports.
6) Deliver random acts of kindness.
7) Bring people together at your home who could benefit from meeting each other.
8) Mentor somebody at work (you never know where they might end up someday).
9) Be a walking Rolodex, and help people find what they need.
10) Acknowledge birthdays and anniversaries, even at work.
11) Never make anyone feel guilty.
12) Support others' successes fully, even if you envy them.

13) Make people more important than anything else.

14) Keep your promises.

15) Send people a note or a card when they're down.

Remember, it's a fine line you walk. Be careful of becoming too nice and being taken advantage of. Also, be aware of being overwhelmed by how many people want a piece of you once you become this generous and irresistible. If you are choosy as to whom you allow into your circle and then focus on having energy-exchange quality relationships, you will be facilitating your way to the top and feeling great about yourself while you're at it.

PARTNERSHIPS

Business partnership has a huge impact on your success and the quality of your life, and yet people spend more time deciding what kind of car to buy than they do choosing the right partner. Most partnerships fail, although the business doesn't always close down. People spend years in dissatisfying partnerships just to keep the business alive. This relationship often starts at the energy-exchange level. Both people feel sparks flying, and they are excited about getting a venture off the ground. Once they are settled in, they create an energy dependence, just floating along. Things get taken for granted, resentments start, and before you know it the partners have become energy drains on each other. Unfortunately, this sounds like many romantic partnerships too. What are you going to do about it? Whether you'd like to put effort into saving a partnership or are thinking

about starting one down the line, here are some basic guidelines to put in place:

1) **After "Who?," "Why?" is the next question.** Understand
clearly why you want to be someone's partner. What does the
other person provide that fills a gap for you? Make sure you understand each other's expectations.

2) **Know who you're dealing with, *really.*** Make sure you know
the person well enough to know if your integrity levels match.
(There is nothing worse than finding out once it's too late that
you have a cheater for a partner.)

3) **Leave nothing to chance.** Have a partnership agreement that
covers all what-ifs and spells out clearly how you can get out of
the partnership and what you take with you if you go. (Don't
kid yourself that you're friends and don't need this, especially if
you value the friendship at all.)

4) ***Vive la différence!*** Focus on strengths. Don't try to make
your partner into you. You were attracted to your partner for
something you didn't have. Honor that; don't punish your partner for it. If one partner is good at networking and the other at
backroom details, celebrate your differences instead of getting
resentful that you bring in all the business. You wouldn't want
to have to do the detail work anyway, and that is worth a lot to
the partnership.

5) **Give each other breathing room.** Allow each person to grow
in the relationship. Partners so often depend on all the variables'
staying the same to be able to count on each other, but entrepreneurs never stay the same. That's your talent, so don't hold
each other back, but do keep the business's best interests at

heart. How can you incorporate new interests or a new direction for the business?

6) Talk! Communicate a lot and evaluate each partner's needs often.

7) "Know when to hold 'em, know when to fold 'em." Know when it's time to go your separate ways, and don't be afraid to follow through.

Emily and Joe were linked romantically and thought it would be a great idea to start a graphic design and communications business together. She was a smart businesswoman and a good writer, and he was technically savvy with computer graphics and desktop publishing. They jumped in without looking and without having a plan or an agreement as to who would do what. Emily assumed the lead and worked hard to get the business off the ground. Joe wasn't particularly inclined to join her in that part, so he didn't have much to do until they got some business coming in. By the time they came to me for coaching, they weren't sure if they should stay in business together or even proceed with their wedding plans.

It was clear that they had completely different expectations of what it meant to be partners in the business. She wanted an equal partner, meaning someone who would share the work load fifty-fifty. He wanted to be a part of her business and make money doing what he was good at, but he didn't really want all the headaches that came with running a business. It took them a couple of months to understand this simple difference between them. The coaching helped them see it, and then we set out to create a structure that would work for both of them.

Emily decided that she still wanted her own business. She

and Joe dissolved the current partnership, and she started a sole proprietorship. She used Joe as an independent contractor to do the computer and design work that she needed, and he supplemented his income by doing the same thing for other people until she had enough business to sustain them both. This small change dissolved all the tension. Her expectations of Joe were now more appropriate to how he could participate. As things got better, their romance got back on track, and before long I received an invitation to their wedding.

ENVY

It just doesn't seem right to end this chapter on relationships without mentioning one of the major culprits in their derailment: envy. (I'm assuming you are not ravaged by jealousy.)

Oh, 'fess up. I know you have been on one side or the other of the mean green demon. It feels terrible, regardless of which side you are on. Whether you are envious of someone else or someone else is envious of you, it just does not feel good. Period.

The only way out of envy is truth and action, which makes it a perfect coaching issue. Don't stew in it. *Do* something about it.

If It's You

If envy is getting the best of you, tell on yourself. Tell the person you envy, or tell someone else. This will get the poison out so you can start to get into action about it.

Envy tells you that someone is doing something or has something that you want to accomplish or obtain for yourself. Yet somewhere in your psyche it has become painful because you made up a story that you can't have it or you're not good enough. Envy is a nasty emotion, so what can you do about it? Recognize that what you are envious of spotlights a need that is not being met for you. Can you identify it? Often, you'll find yourself envious of someone for something that you really wouldn't want for yourself, so why is it eating at you? A friend may get a great new job with more money, a better title, some nice perks, and a move to a desirable part of the country. Now, what are you envious of? If you don't want to move and you wouldn't want that kind of responsibility, why do you still feel envious? Maybe this person's good fortune is reminding you that you would like to make more money or that you too are ready for a change.

Can you see the bottom line here? Envy is a call to action. It is really saying, "Get off your butt and get what you want." So the next time you are struck by the mean green demon, don't waste your energy wishing someone else ill or whining about your misfortune. Recognize it as a sign that you need to get into action, and change what is no longer OK with you.

If It's Someone Else

It doesn't feel any better to have envy directed at you than it does to feel it yourself. You may find yourself pulling away from people or even hiding your accomplishments in order to not make anyone else feel bad. Don't do it. You have two choices: You can look for people who can handle your success, or you can remind your friends or colleagues that if you can do it, they can too. It's easy to be generous when you are out in front. Use this opportunity to remind others that envy is a call to action.

What do they need to do to join you where you are? Give them ideas and support. If you're not ready to be that generous, at least be graceful and don't use the fact that you know someone is envious as a weapon.

Relationships of every kind and at every level will affect your journey to the top. You can take action to get relationships to be another factor in your success instead of being a hindrance to it. Each one is a test of your own mettle. Will you stretch to make a relationship work? Will the stretch be finally putting an end to one that doesn't work? Who will you become, as you now know what to look for in relationships? Will you still let people drain you? Will the status quo be enough? Will you find those relationships that rocket you to the top? Just remember, you attract the relationships you are ready for, so do whatever you have to do to be ready for the powerful ones.

Relationships are the vehicle that usher in your success.

Make your vehicle the top of the line.

Ensure Quality Relationships
That Can Rocket You to the Top

▼

1. Identify what kind of relationships you keep now (energy-draining, energy-dependent, or energy-exchange).
2. Refocus all your relationships to the energy-exchange level.

3. Develop your inside ten.
4. Develop and nurture your frontline twenty.
5. Deal with people by being of service.
6. If you are a partner, be a good partner.
7. Refocus envy into a positive emotion.
8. Let your relationships rocket you to the top!

FOURTEEN

▼

Advanced Tools for
Getting to the Top

I F YOU'VE ALLOWED YOURSELF TO BE COACHED WHILE READING this book, if you've taken action, and if you've shifted your mind-set, you should be starting to see changes in your personal and professional life. Now you are ready to hear about some concepts and tools that will stretch you to reach for even more. We've focused on the nuts and bolts and figured out how to move certain situations to a more positive plateau. Now it's time to explore more ways to take you to the top of your game. Each concept is a window through which to examine your desires, which will help you to make them come true. You can use them all, but you're more likely to find one that rings true for you and that you would like to assimilate. Look at each one as something to attain. If you don't get it, don't worry about it. If you find yourself resistant to it, ask yourself why. If it doesn't appeal to you, ignore it, and if it lights you up, put it at the fore-front of your mind and let it paint a whole new picture for you. You'll assimilate each concept as you're ready for it.

INTENTION

The dictionary defines *intention* as an aim that guides action. How do you apply that to your career and your life? You'll have to understand that what you intend, what you truly focus your energy on, will, in some form, come to be. If you've ever experienced great luck, something occurring out of nowhere at great benefit to you, think about what you were positively focusing on around the time of that event. Maybe it wasn't as out of the blue as you remembered. Maybe you were intending it to happen. Your intention can be that powerful. Am I saying that you can just think about things, and boom, they occur? Yes, I suppose I am, but it is definitely a skill to be developed. If you think it's baloney, you won't be able to do it. Your intention is that it can't work, so why should it? Am I asking you to believe in magic? Maybe a little bit.

Think of this in another way, and you'll see how powerful it is. Have you ever gossiped? Someone walks out of the room, and you immediately start spewing underhanded comments or jokes, commenting on that person in some way. What is your intention? Not a pretty one, I hate to say. The next time you see that person, you act quite pleasant. They seem distant, and this annoys you even more. Did you really think that they have no idea of what your intention is? Your hidden intentions are just as powerful as your overt ones. That person was distant because, consciously or not, the object of your gossip knew you could not be trusted 100 percent. Whichever side you've been on in this scenario, you have experienced the power of intention. Can you imagine using that power as a focused tool to get you where you want to go? Watch out, world, here you come.

When Britt, the executive VP turned national director of sales operations, found herself after a merger with a new boss who came from the other company, she was bitter and dissatisfied not with him personally, but rather with the circumstances that brought him in. Her original intention, whether she realized it or not, was to let him sink or swim of his own accord. When she switched her intention to becoming his ally, her actions changed. She found ways to be in touch with him more often and did all she could to help him. She did not do this to get anything or to be manipulative. It just felt like a better way to go. Lo and behold, as you already know, it got her a huge promotion.

Fran was a housewife with no business experience. Through a series of events in her own life, she developed a passion for teaching children exercise at an early age. She influenced her own kids with this passion, but she felt it needed another outlet. With no experience and no clue as to where to begin, she decided to make an exercise video for kids and use it to get the word out about her cause. Over time, with consistent action, each piece fell into place, until she had developed a lucrative business that included videos, speaking engagements, and opportunities to be published. She became an authority on children's fitness. She had nothing to go on but her intention to have people hear her message.

My story is similar. For at least ten years of my adolescent-to-adult life, I could remember my father being unhappy with his work. Even in his worst moments, my father could not see his way to making a change. When I found myself in a similar situation in one of my work experiences, it hit me that no one was meant to exist this way. There had to be work and a life that was perfect for each person. I believed that deeply, but I wasn't really sure what to do about it. During my years as a professional actress, I knew that I wanted to have an impact on people's lives. I hoped that they would see a character I played or a performance I was in that somehow inspired them to change their own lives.

When I realized I didn't have to stay in such a difficult business to have that impact, I began using acting techniques as a way to train people to communicate better so they could advance their careers. When I found the profession of coaching, I knew I had run into the expression of my deepest beliefs. People *can* have it all. You can have work and a life you love inside and out. Fifteen years and hundreds of clients later, you are reading my first book. Could I have told you I would be doing this with my life? Was it part of my plan? No. So what got me here? Intention. I always *intended* to find a way for myself and others to have an extraordinary life.

So what's the rub? Why isn't this automatic for everyone? For starters, take responsibility for what you intend. As long as you keep being responsible for what is on your plate, getting rid of the bad and taking great care of the good, the road to the horizon you choose should be straight. If bumps arise, this will be your chance to find the hidden opportunity that may be the key to your intentions finding their realization in your life.

DETACHMENT

When you want something very badly, you can get so wrapped up in it that you can't see anything else; you are attached to a result. It has to come true or your whole world will fall apart. Could you make it harder to achieve your goals? I don't think so. If you're struggling, now you know why. You are too hooked in to the result you crave. Practicing detachment will make the process of achieving your goals a lot easier.

"But how do I have great passion and intention for something, take action in that direction, and not be invested in its coming to fruition?" That's what I hear you asking. Good question. It's a fine line that reflects the duality of everything in life. I don't want to contradict myself here. Do everything we've talked about: take action, expect the best to happen, be specific about what you want, AND develop the ability to leave it alone to see what happens. It's like planting a garden. You till the soil, choose the seeds, wait for the right moment to plant, nurture the plants with great care, and then walk away to let them grow. You can't do the growing. You can only do what you know to do and leave the garden to do what it does.

The same goes for your personal and professional goals. If you stand over them every moment, willing them to happen, you'll wear yourself out and block the sunlight they need. Get out of the way and enjoy your life, and if the seeds you planted don't take root, try something else.

Robin had been working herself up for weeks to ask her boss for a raise. We had been strategizing a plan, but she seemed to get increasingly more anxious instead of feeling better prepared and more relaxed. She had created a scenario in her mind that if this raise request did not go exactly as she had hoped, her life would be ruined. She was becoming more and more attached to having this conversation going her way. She became almost defiant as she built her case for deserving a raise. Anger was filtering through. If she didn't find a way to be detached from whatever result came from this meeting, it would be a self-fulfilling prophecy and be disastrous.

Robin was able to be more open to whatever would happen in that meeting once we spelled out all the options she had if she didn't get the raise she wanted. Only then did she set up the meeting. Her boss was glad that Robin had broached the subject, because she had something in mind for her that she had not had time to bring up before. Her boss was considering creating a whole new position that she thought Robin would be perfect for. Not only would this position mean more money, but it would also include transitioning into a new aspect of the business that she was interested in, with great future possibilities. It was more than she had ever expected to happen.

What if Robin had remained resentful and hell-bent on getting the raise the way she had originally planned? Of course, we have no real way of knowing, but I would venture to say that her anger might have made her boss see a side of Robin that caused her to change her mind about the new position. I am speculating, but I've seen this enough to say it's a sound possibility. Her detachment allowed her to be open to whatever happened and to adjust her approach and her needs from there.

BEYOND GOALS

What if I told you that once you've worked so hard to get it all together, you may reach a time when you stop having goals? You may reach a point where you don't know what goals to set anymore; you will feel almost like you're slipping backward because you used to be so fanatic about goals and structure. You may just feel like you no longer have any discipline at all. Don't panic.

Goals are like training wheels. You need them to learn how to ride a bike, but eventually you take them off. When you went to get your driver's license, you were a student driver with a permit and supervision, but soon, you were on your own. Goals work much the same way. You need them to focus you and direct you and usher you to a desired result. Then it's time for progress. There are always bigger goals to set, but I just want to warn you that somewhere along your path you may give up having goals altogether. It's a very organic decision. You can't force it, or you will slip backward. When you really are at the stage where you become goalless, it will propel you forward, not send you back to square one. You will begin to naturally respond to what occurs. You may go in and out of needing linear goals and not needing them. Not to worry. As you climb to each level of success, you may need to put the training wheels back on for a brushup.

Goallessness leaves you with enough room to create some other criteria for keeping yourself moving forward. This is where it gets to be fun. Your criteria will now be nonlinear. There may or may not be any logic in the way those criteria will help you accomplish more. But logic is not our goal here; our goal is to expand your thinking and to bring in more success at less emotional cost. The last time I went through a goalless stage, I stopped running my business in all linear, logical steps and focused on the nonlinear criteria of delight. Every client I worked with had to be a delight, every group I spoke for had to be a delight, every organization I was involved with, every task I touched, and every person I came in contact with, down to the lady at the post office window. Over the course of six months I stepped down as president of a networking organization, hired a bookkeeper because I hated doing my own business books, moved to a much nicer location, and—as it happened—I doubled my business, all as a result of following my nonlinear criteria. Goals were out. Delight was in.

My clients have played with such nonlinear criteria as: It has to be fun, it has to be something I haven't done before, it must afford me freedom, it has to be a ridiculously high amount of money, it has to make a great impact, it has to be an adventure, and the work must be only in great locations. You may find that your nonlinear criteria are limited, but don't let that stop you from giving it a try. To be someone who can create and rely on a steady stream of business, career, and life opportunities, you will need to experiment with nonlinear criteria. If you become goalless, you can avoid burnout whenever life becomes busier. You can weed out what can stay and what must go, as well as adding some variety.

When Jeanine decided to go goalless, she used a nonlinear guideline that I introduce to all of my clients at one time or another. That guideline led her to find a way of attracting business and opportunities instead of working so hard to get them. She stopped all her usual, logical ways of going after business. She

stopped cold calling, she stopped mailings, she stopped schmoozing. Instead, she thought of ways to bring her clients to her. She
did free demonstrations of what her company offered. She
spent time with people getting to know them, and didn't worry
about doing business. She went out of her way to educate her
clients on topics that were of relevance to them, and did not
necessarily sell her product. In eight months, her business went
up by 30 percent. It all came to her. No pushing, no hard sell.
Instead, she drew it all to her like a magnet. It was not necessarily logical that business would come to her if she stopped
selling, but she knew she couldn't work that hard anymore. She
declared that business had to come to her. She took the appropriate action, and she found a much easier way to be successful.

Do you think you're ready for this? Are you having a strong
reaction to what I'm saying? Do you think it's impossible? Do
you think it's too good to be true? Are you wondering why you
didn't start playing this way sooner? It's your choice. It always
has been. Is it going to be hard, or is it going to be fun? It's up to
you. Remember, you can only go goalless if you already are in a
good place. Otherwise, you need those goals to bridge you over
to success. It's a matter of style and how you do best. It's not an
excuse to get lazy or irresponsible and claim you've gone goalless. If your life is not working, you are not ready to be goalless.
It's something you earn and graduate to once things have been
consistently good for so long that goals become a bore.

LEGACY

Living their lives to create a legacy is something that most people don't achieve in their lifetime. They are too busy surviving.

Yet this is an advanced, unusual way to define your business and personal success. It demands that you think beyond your own needs and devote your efforts to the needs of others. It is often that broader scope that facilitates being successful. Some people do better when they are striving to succeed at something bigger than themselves.

You don't have to sacrifice to leave a legacy or do it solely for altruistic reasons. It's just an expression of your reaching further than most people go. Stephen Covey, well-respected consultant, speaker, author, and spiritual/business authority, is an example of living a legacy that is also a profitable business venture. He has created systems, documents, tools, and concepts that people will use for years to come that express what he sees possible for companies and families in terms of living and working to our highest capacity. People's lives will change because of the tools he has given them and because of what he has chosen to devote his life to.

On the altruistic side, Pamela had become so successful in her career as a fashion designer that she was feeling somewhat bored. This client had all the material things she could ever want, she derived great satisfaction from her work and relationships, and yet she couldn't help but feel that there was something missing. Directing her thoughts to creating a legacy sparked her motivation to do something she had dreamed about for a long time.

Pamela had come from an abusive home where her mother suffered greatly. She had always wished there was someplace where her mother could have tapped into resources to become more independent and someday walk away from the trap she was in. Her mother had long since passed away, but Pamela felt that a nonprofit group that provided counseling, job training, life training, and financial assistance would contribute to help-ing other women avoid what her mother had endured so long ago.

She attained nonprofit status, applied for funding, and hired the right people to run the organization. Her visibility in the fashion industry made it easier to attract support and money. Turning her attention away from her business temporarily did not hurt it at all. In fact, it helped. Her work was respected even more when people knew about the cause she supported. She had a hand in changing many lives, and she was leaving some-thing that might outlive her.

Everything you do has an impact and affects other people's lives in one way or another, so really, there is a legacy to each one of us. However, if you want to take it to an extraordinary level, it's a whole other way to live your life. What about your legacy? Is there something that needs to be said? Is there some-thing you see that could make a difference if it were done? Now is the time to reflect for a moment on what it would mean to have that level of impact. What can you change right now with even the slightest effort to play at this level? Nonetheless, no matter how you play this, remember that your greatest legacy is being an example of a life that is working. That is your first legacy. Now take yourself to the next level. There is no time like the present to begin.

CHOICES

If we accomplish anything together, let it be that you can see that you always have a choice. The choices you make weave the

fiber of your life. You choose the people, you choose your out-
look, you choose your situations. Your career and life unfold,
reflecting those choices. Yes, many things are put in your path,
but you can choose how you deal with those too. How you
choose to operate in your career will have a huge impact on
your life. People tend to think they have less ability to choose in
career, job, and work. That is not true. Granted, there may be
unwanted consequences to some choices, but choosing what is
right for you when it comes from an unadulterated, clear place
(rather than your ego) will bring you to what you want. Make
choices that fuel you. Stop making choices that kill you bit
by bit.

Every choice you make is rooted either in fear or in courage.
It's that simple. If you break it down to that common denomi-
nator, you will have access to simple decisions. You will know
when you are cheating yourself and when you are being your
own champion. If a choice is rooted in fear, it's bound to de-
stroy something or someone, even in the subtlest way. If you
follow the more courageous choice, you are putting your best
foot forward.

These examples will give you a clearer picture:

Fear	Courage
Feeling a lack in some way	Expecting the best for yourself
Feeling jealous or envious	Being the bigger person
Abusing power	Being compassionate
Being irresponsible	Expecting more from yourself
Being pessimistic	Being optimistic
Being self-deprecating	Being your own advocate

It takes great awareness to be conscious of the common de-nominator of any choice you make. However, if you have adopted some of the work of this book, you should be simpli-fying and slowing down the speed of your everyday existence enough to have the presence of mind to do so. Dissect every de-cision and find its root in fear or courage, and make the choices that will ultimately serve you best.

Dale was a senior manager at one of the top technology com-panies in the country when she came to work with me on im-proving her leadership style. She had inherited her organization from someone who had been her boss and had since moved on. She found herself immediately taking on his way of doing things in order to keep consistency in the changeover; however, his style was totally unnatural to her, and yet she was unsure how to turn it around. She wasn't even sure what choices she had because she had done it his way so long as one of his man-agers. She felt out of control, which started to reflect in the de-partment, and word was coming back that she was ineffective as a manager. She was feeling the heat and knew it was time to do something when she picked up the phone and called me.

The quickest way to start making changes was to map out what choices she was being confronted with. She needed to get her stress level down so she had the clarity to focus her efforts on improving the situation. The fearful choice would have been to continue to ignore herself and her health in order to look good to the organization, and to keep juggling more than she could. She delegated and streamlined her responsibilities so she could focus on what was really important, a choice that started leading to resolution.

Second, she recognized that she had to develop her own

strength in order to stop relying on the power-wielding ways she had learned from her autocratic ex-boss. She realized that abusing her power was the small-minded, fear-based way to go. She accomplished more by choosing to clearly communicate the goals and expectations she had for each person and the department, and she encouraged each person to achieve them.

Finally, she had to retrain her salespeople to stop inching forward and start building critical mass through better relationship building, to develop her business to the target level. She knew her fearful choice was to leave things as they were, so she chose instead to make the effort to redirect her staff. She put them through rigorous training and had weekly progress meetings to reinforce the improvements. When her choices were clear, she could see her way to the solutions, step-by-step. When she understood that the choices that held her back were rooted in fear, and that those that propelled her forward were based in courage, she stopped taking a long time to make decisions of any magnitude.

The choices you make will determine how quickly you move toward the top and how easy it will be to get there. No more playing small. Choose to have a great life and great career success. Don't be afraid to ask for it and even sometimes demand it, but from a position of strength, not by an abuse of power. What are the choices you can stand to make to take you to the next level? In every moment, you can choose. Choose well. Choose to be on your own side. Choose to think big. Be ready to be responsible for what your choices create, but don't be afraid to go for it.

What you intend, you create.

Advanced Skills to Use As You're Ready

▼

1. Have clear intentions.
2. Practice being detached from results.
3. Become goalless.
4. Create a legacy.
5. Choose wisely.
6. Welcome to the top!

FIFTEEN

▼

Put On Your Seatbelts—
Here Comes the Future

TAKING YOURSELF TO THE TOP—THAT GAME IS NEVER-ENDING. As you reach beyond what you thought possible, you are ready for the next horizon to set your sights on. It's human nature. It's how we challenge ourselves to grow. Having some context in which to set that next horizon will help you get there. The work you have done has set you up well for adapting to the future that you want to attract. What's next? We have entered a new century. How will it be for those of us living and working in 2015 and 2030 or beyond? The current trend for people wanting to attain a higher quality of life and making changes in how they work will not stop. It will evolve to higher and higher versions of itself. You will no longer be planning your life and career, but rather designing them, truly letting choice be the palette from which you paint how you work and live. You will be changing how things get done from the inside out instead of bowing to the circumstances set up by our society and corporations as to how you should work and live. For some, this is a revolution; for others, just a natural evolution. You will express who you are through how you work and live. If you can't do that through a big company, you'll do it by going out on your own. If you're already on your own, you'll keep finding ways to do it your way and be a trendsetter for everyone else.

In our work together you've prepared yourself to take this on. You've stretched, you've invested in your ability to achieve more, you've elevated your performance and raised your expectations of yourself, your career, and your life. You now demand more than ever before of your time on the planet. You want meaningful work and substance to your life. To sustain what we have built here, you'll need to:

1) Keep unacceptable things from building up in your life.
2) Stop underestimating yourself.
3) Live what matters to you most.
4) Connect with people on a deeper level than you have before.
5) Keep in touch with who you are so you can keep success coming on your own terms.

It is no longer theory, but rather factual truth that we are the entrepreneurs of our own careers. We live in the Age of Entrepreneurism. Whether self-employed or corporately employed, we are all being asked to be responsible for ourselves. The old contract of being recruited by a company at a young age and being a loyal employee for a working lifetime is not available anymore. And it seems at this point, we wouldn't want it even if it was.

Furthermore, as our trust in organizations has diminished because of corruption and lack of loyalty, it becomes critical to become more self-directed. We can no longer rely on the organizations and institutions in our lives to show us how to live. We have to be more self-referenced to succeed. That means being very clear on who you are and what you can do (not to mention what you want too). This clarity also assumes that you know your function and purpose in the grander scheme of a business. As people evolve and recognize that there is something they do better than anyone else, and as they (and you) make your work an expression of it, competition will decrease. At the very least, you won't perceive that there is competition because you will understand your intrinsic value. There will be no need to reinvent to compete, you'll only need to tune in to what's already there. And like many, you may find that what is already in there requires working on your own to be expressed. It's OK. You will not be alone. Small business is big business and you'll be in the same boat as millions of others.

Where does coaching fit into all this? Coaching is growing at such a rapid rate that it is becoming as common to have a coach as it is to have an accountant. It is not a trend. It is here to stay until it's not needed anymore. Large companies have caught on, hiring experienced coaches to train people to become what will be an internal team of coaches, as well as training their managers to adopt coaching as their management style. Coaching will become the only way for managers to keep up with the demands of their own jobs and constantly improve performance of their teams and staff. They will need to know people well and learn how to coach. It is already proving to be marvelously effective.

People will continue to hire coaches on an individual basis to keep themselves fresh and constantly upgrade their careers and lives. Corporate managers and executives will rely on coaching to help them become more and more portable and marketable. You will use them to become better leaders, removing the defects from your business and life as well as assimilating the coaching skills to use with your people. Or you'll use them to help you make the leap into your own business. The entrepreneur and business owner will use their coach to continue filtering all the information that keeps coming at them at faster and faster rates, in order to stay viable in the marketplace. Even more important, they'll rely on their coach to help them discover new ways to be successful without a high emotional cost.

By doing the work in this book you have kicked off your journey into this future. You are well prepared; just don't let the work stop here. Keep going. Make time to make improvements on an ongoing basis. Don't wait for a crisis before you start doing something.

As I said at the beginning, no one is supposed to suffer to make a living. What is and will continue to be the biggest change in how we lead our lives is our insistence that we be happy at work. It used to be a ridiculous notion. Hard work and sacrifice to provide were the norm. But we have evolved and we want more. We want meaning and we want to like what we do and we want to have a life! Even in tougher times, when we think we do not have the luxury of making a change to be more satisfied, it will still be the beacon of hope for the worker. Whether it is simplifying your own business or bringing a sharper focus to your role in a company, a constant evolution will need to be allowed to occur as our world keeps changing at a faster and faster rate.

You have learned long-lasting tools here that will help you forge your way. It's no mistake that you've let a coach come along and guide you. You are ready whether you think you are or not. You would not have picked up this book if you weren't ready for what it had to say. There is no time like the present to take action. What does it cost you not to make a change? What is the cost to your family and your overall happiness? What would it feel like to settle? I know you don't want to do that. What I want for you is a successful career AND a great life. Let no limits stop you. You'll know when you've reached the top.

> There is always room at the top.
> —Daniel Webster

How to Choose a Coach

I F YOU ARE CONSIDERING HIRING A COACH, THERE ARE MANY TO choose from, and the number is growing quickly as the profession expands. These questions and guidelines will help you find the right coach.

- Rapport is very important. In the initial consultation you should feel confident that you've found someone you can trust and be happy to have as a partner in your success.
- Location is normally not important. While some coaches do exclusively on-site coaching, it is not necessary to getting results. You'll get the same or better results with telephone coaching at a fraction of the cost of on-site visits.
- Ask questions about the coach's depth of experience, years of training, credentials (if any), background previous to being a coach and successes in the areas in which you seek

assistance. Look for someone who has had coach-specific training and has been credentialed.

- Many companies will now pay for coaching as they pay for other training and seminars you'd like to attend. Consider which companies have employed your prospective coach.
- Don't be afraid to ask a coach for client referrals.
- Speak to more than one coach before you decide. Get a feel for who is the best fit, and then trust yourself to choose well.

Here are some questions to ask:

- What is your coaching philosophy? (They vary quite a bit.)
- Have you had experience with people in my situation?
- How long do clients typically work with you?
- What would a coaching package with you include?
- How do you handle confidentiality and reporting back to my company?
- In your opinion, when does coaching not work?
- What do you feel is your specialty as a coach?
- Would you refer me to someone else if another specialty were needed?

What you can expect in the first few sessions:

- Assessing where you are and where you'd like to be
- In a corporate setting, assessing the goals the company has for your coaching in relation to your own
- Setting specific goals and benchmarks for the coaching

What you can expect to be ongoing:

- There is no curriculum. Coaching is a client-initiated agenda.
- Continuous follow-up on the issues and goals of the coaching
- Instruction, discussion, and guidance toward your objectives
- Homework
- A source of continuous positive support

APPENDIX B

Coaching Resources and Referral Sources

For information on the profession and referral services, you can contact the industry's leading professional association:

International Coach Federation®
1444 I Street NW
Suite 700
Washington, DC 20005
Phone: (888) 423-3131 or (202) 712-9039
Fax: (888) 329-2423 or (202) 216-9646
E-mail: *icfoffice[at]coachfederation.org*

Other:
Professional Coaches and Mentors Association (PCMA)
Phone: (800) 979-7262
E-mail: *info@pcmaonline.com*

For information on becoming a coach or further assistance in finding a coach, you can contact one of the following coach-training institutions:

Coach University (CoachU)
PO Box 881595
Steamboat Springs, CO 80488-1595
Phone: (800) 48COACH (toll-free)
Fax: (800) 329-5655
Web site: *www.coachu.com*
E-mail: *admissions@coachu.com*
Contact: Sandy Vilas

The Coaches Training Institute (CTI)
1879 Second Street
San Rafael, CA 94901
Phone: (415) 451-6000; (800) 691-6008 (toll free)
Fax: (415) 460-6878
E-mail: *info@thecoaches.com*
Web site: *www.thecoaches.com*
Contact: Giles MacMillan

Institute for Life Coach Training
(formerly Therapist University)
Dr. Patrick Williams, Ed.D., M.C.C. (president)
Ms. Edwina Adams (administrator)
2801 Wakonda Drive
Ft. Collins, Colorado 80521
Phone: (972) 867-1915
Fax: (972) 867-2063
E-mail: *info@lifecoachtraining.com*
Web site: *www.lifecoachtraining.com*

The Newfield Network
2804 Fountain Grove Terrace
Olney, MD 20832
Phone: (301) 570-6680
Fax: (301) 570-5765
E-mail: Terrie Lupberger
Web site: *www.newfieldnetwork.com*
Contact: Terrie Lupberger

About the Author

LAURA BERMAN FORTGANG is internationally recognized as a pioneer in the personal coaching field and is the best-selling author of *Living Your Best Life* and *Now What?: 90 Days to a New Life Direction*. *Take Yourself to the Top* was the first published work by a personal coach in the United States.

As a trendsetting leader in both lifestyle and corporate forums, Laura is often featured on national television as well as in international print and digital media. Her appearances on *Oprah*, the CBS *Early Show*, NBC's *Weekend Today*, MSNBC, CNBC, CNN, and dozens of others, combined with print media such as *USA Today*, *Fast Company*, *Money*, and multiple national and international newspapers have paved the way for many of the most successful coaches in the industry today.

Through her coaching company, LBF*InterCoach, Inc., and its new division, The Life Blueprint™ Institute, Laura has provided coaching to diverse groups of clients ranging from homemakers, celebrities, and Fortune 500 companies to NASA and the Army Corps of Engineers. She is a popular and dynamic speaker whose style translates across cultures, and her books are published in eleven languages and distributed around the world. Laura is currently a contributing editor and columnist for *Redbook* magazine.

One of the first recipients of the International Coach Federations's Master Coach credential, Laura was a founding member of ICF and a four-year board member, and has been a tireless champion for the coaching profession around the world.

Laura is a "Jersey Girl," a devoted spouse, and the mother of three kids.

Laura Berman Fortgang is available for keynote presentations, workshops, and seminars. Her team of coaches are available to help with your one-on-one coaching needs.

InterCoach, Inc., and The Life Blueprint™ Institute
26 Park Street, Suite 2045
Montclair, New Jersey 07042
(973) 857-8180
(888) 23-COACH

For our free newsletter, send an e-mail to *subscribe@inter-coach.com.*

Take free quizzes and find out more about products and services at *www.laurabermanfortgang.com* and *www.inter-coach.com.*